Run To Faith

James Deren

Grey Wolfe Publishing, LLC
PO Box 1088
Birmingham, Michigan 48009
www.GreyWolfePublishing.com

© 2015 James Deren
Published by Grey Wolfe Publishing, LLC
www.GreyWolfePublishing.com
All Rights Reserved

ISBN: 978-1628280739
Library of Congress Control Number: 2015933440

Run To Faith

The Journey to Athletic and Spiritual Contentment

James Deren

Acknowledgements

The inspiration for this book was formulated through the relationships of believers and non-believers who have impacted me throughout my life in my quest for spiritual and athletic contentment.

I would especially like to thank my daughter, Renee Ratliff who inspired me by supporting the stories and experiences that I have shared with her while growing up. She provided that gentle push... to put my experiences on paper and share them to inspire others.

For my wife Debbie, who is always there for both spiritual and athletic support, setting a great example by putting God and others first.

For my daughters Rose and Rachel who have grown to enjoy every moment as they live their lives for Almighty God.

For that special team of distance runners at Eastern Michigan University in the mid-1970s who provided inspiration through their performances on the track, but more importantly, became my best friends and continue to be a big part of my life today.

For Coach Bob Parks who through his kindness created a family around that special EMU team, by giving me a chance to develop and be the best I could be.

For the leaders and members of Grace Church in White Lake, Michigan who provided thought leadership and taught me to strive to understand the Word of God.

And to Jesus Christ, my Savior, who provided the ultimate sacrifice in order to ensure that we gain eternal life and contentment.

The secret to happiness:

"Happiness is attained not through what you have but through who you are and what you do."

Contents

Contentment

"And God said, "Behold, I have given you every plant-yielding seed that is on the face of all the earth, and every tree with seed in its fruit. You shall have them for food. And to every beast of the earth and to every bird of the heavens and to everything that creeps on the earth, everything that has the breath of life, I have given every green plant for food." And it was so. And God saw everything that He had made, and behold, it was very good." Genesis 1: 29-31

"Every moment on this Earth is a gift from God." The thought resonated in my mind as I contemplated the answer to a question recently posed to me. "How does it feel?" The question was prompted by two significant recent events: my 60th birthday and the birth of my first grandson. The unspoken rest of the question would be "...to be old", which was inferred from these recent events. Contemplating my answer, I realized that turning sixty, or being a grandparent, is remarkably different and not what my younger-self I had envisioned. My view of sixty had been formulated primarily through my lifestyle observations of my parents, grandparents, uncles and aunts. Based on my observations, I envisioned and expected a lifestyle that was mainly sedentary and serious. As a youth, my older relatives appeared to be a wise and serious group whose lifestyle and personality were defined by their work ethics—on the job and at home. In their spare time, they enjoyed eating, drinking and visiting one another. The men participated in group functions including hunting, fishing, bowling, and coaching little-league baseball. The women, who had little of the conveniences we enjoy today, were consumed with cooking, shopping, cleaning, laundry, and transporting us children to our activities. My uncles also found time to learn musical instruments. This skill resulted in countless hours of playing polka for fun as well as for organized events. In those days there seemed to be little time or interest in the types of recreational activities that are a major part of my current lifestyle. Activities such as running, swimming, hiking, and camping were thought to be reserved for the younger generation.

Times have changed, according to the popular adage "sixty is the new forty". There is no question that the body slows down-my chronic aches and pains remind me. I have a dramatic loss of flexibility and running efficiency, as well as total dependence on reading glasses whenever I use a computer or look at printed materials. I occasionally experience the well-known senior moments when I forget why I enter a room or can't recall a recent conversation. However, many of the things I enjoy remain. I love the feeling of running a fast 200-yard sprint or pushing through a good workout. I love the smell and taste of Thanksgiving Dinner or a dish of ice-cream. The sights and smells of nature have not changed and I still enjoy and cherish God's world.

I thought about the question and I asked myself: "What age would I rather be?" As a youngster, I enjoyed the freedom of playtime, experiencing new adventures and places for the first time, making new friends and my youthful athleticism. Then I thought about the downside. I remember the nervousness of a first date; the total dependence on my parents for essentials such as food, shelter, and clothing; the stress that comes with trying to fit into my peer group. I remember countless hours of studying and worrying about grades, exams, and job interviews. Freedom was offset by the need to keep a car running and pay the rent while earning minimum wage. I then recalled the memories and experiences that have led me to where I am today: the joy of winning my first race; graduating college; landing my first job; earning a promotion; meeting and marrying my wife; the birth of my children; my spiritual growth as a believer and follower of Jesus Christ. I realized these are memories that I cherish and despite some hardships along the way, would not want to erase.

A number of recent, popular movies focus on a plot where a character is transformed into their past and given an opportunity to re-live their youth and change their past. What seems like fun at first, ultimately changes history so that their future personality is not who they had worked to become. Remember Marty McFly who found he had to undo the events that he had changed to have a future? The book and movie "The Seven People You Meet in Heaven" illustrates the results of our decisions and actions and the unknown impact we have on the lives of others. Despite any regrets we may have about our past course of action, we need to remember that both the good and the bad experiences have led us to where and who we are today.

The past helps me appreciate the person I am today. With each day, I find contentment by cherishing both the significant and every-day events. I find that my love for my wife, although strong and genuine in our early years of marriage, grows stronger each day. My relationship with my children and close friends is strengthened through the times we share together. Every run, swim, hike, and bike ride becomes an experience that is ingrained into who I am and is forever etched in my memory. My work experiences support my career growth to the point where I can provide insights and solutions to help others more effectively do their jobs. Most importantly, I use my journey to grow as a Christian by drawing nearer to our Savior through prayer, study, and actions.

So what's next? My faith leads me to look forward to my future. I expect to decline in my physical strength and athleticism. I know I will run and swim slower, and be plagued with increasing aches and pains and senior moments. These things, however, are fleeting moments that will matter little when I leave this earth and attain the ultimate goal of living in eternal happiness with our Creator.

"For God so loved the world, that He gave his only Son, that whoever believes in Him should not perish but have eternal life." *John 3:16* As Christians, our faith teaches us that mortality applies to everyone and living forever can only happen if we give our lives to Jesus. Without faith in the promise of Jesus that He will provide us with eternal life would seem purposeless. As much as I have mourned the deaths of my close friends Mark Giblin; Dave Kanners; and John Hanson; my mother and father; and numerous aunts, uncles and neighbors. I rejoice in the faith that they are eternally happy with our creator.   The belief that mortal life is but a moment in the scope of eternity provides the incentive that allows us to embrace, rather than dread, the aging process. We are free to live each moment with full contentment, knowing that God has given us His promise of eternal happiness.

Introduction

"Do you not know that in a race all the runners run, but only one receives the prize? So run that you may obtain it. Every athlete exercises self-control in all things. They do it to receive a perishable wreath, but we are imperishable. So I do not run aimlessly;" 1 Corinthians 9:24-26

The race is down to the three Americans who are moments away from giving the United States their first 1-2-3 finish in the Olympic marathon. Jim Deren, Tom Hollander, and Brian Williams are neck and neck as they enter the Olympic stadium for the final lap on the track. The crowd roars in support as these three are claiming their place in Olympic history."

This was a typical scenario of my training runs at Eastern Michigan University in the 1970's. One of the tricks we used to make long runs more fun was to escape our world for a few moments and let our imagination run wild. These moments are what I remember most about my days as a college distance runner at Eastern. "The three Americans put in a surge at mile twenty-two and dropped the Kenyans. As they approach the finish line they are holding hands and for the first time in Olympic history—a three-way tie for the gold medal!"

In my lifelong search for happiness and contentment, I find running to be a great escape from the problems and every-day pressures of the world. Running rewards me with great pleasure, and often takes me back to the feeling I had as a child when games such as tag, hide and seek, and capture the flag resulted in hours of enjoyment. I use the escape of running to energize and elevate my moods. The places I've seen and adventures that I've uncovered are numerous. Whether it's exploring a new place on a business trip or vacation; leaving the office for my lunch hour; or braving extreme weather by enjoying the outdoors when others dare not venture outside... running makes my life more enjoyable. It provides me with quiet time to solve problems, make decisions, overcome challenges or reflect on life. Running has bestowed upon me the gift of companionship by giving me time with friends and family. It has strengthened my marriage by giving me alone time with my wife. And it has provided me with an outlet for my competitive nature.

I find a similar source of strength and contentment through my spiritual faith as a follower of Jesus Christ. Several years ago I was struggling to find purpose in my career. I found the answer by turning to my heavenly Father. When I lay in bed at the end of that busy day, I closed my eyes and prayed to God. "Dear God, Thank you for all you have given to me. You have provided me with all I need... a great family, good health, good friends and a wonderful home but most of all the gift of eternal life with You." Over the previous few days, I was consumed with an important career decision. My work in the Information Technology field had been steadily advancing for several years and I was at a crossroad. I experienced the most enjoyment and fulfillment working as an analyst and planner for a hospital several years prior, but changes in our corporation led me to my current position in the manufacturing sector. The pay, benefits and career possibilities were excellent and provided adequately for my family, but something was missing. I lacked a sense of purpose and enthusiasm in my role. I was offered a position at a start-up company in the healthcare industry. Was I willing to risk my current comfort level to pursue this opportunity? I thought about how a job change might affect my ability to provide for my family. My financial goals were to maintain my family's lifestyle and to build a college fund for my three daughters. I also wanted to ensure that my wife and I were financially secure for retirement.

While my current position was exciting at first, the newness quickly faded. I had the technical skills. However, I lacked the cultural background that I needed to make a difference and provide me with a sense of purpose. When I made a mental list of pros and cons, I realized that my past work experiences in the healthcare sector taught me a great deal about more than just hospital technology but something that I had undervalued; the people, processes, culture of caregivers, and how hospitals work. More importantly, it gave me a strong sense of purpose knowing that my contributions toward providing timely patient information to caregivers could increase the quality of patient care and potentially save lives.

"Lord, please guide me to make the decision that will allow me to best serve You and provide for others." I felt a sense of peace, remembering that my highest priority in life is to serve and honor God, and whatever happened was a part of His plan for me. I realized whatever the outcome; God would lead me to a decision that was ultimately best for me. I slept knowing I had learned to rely upon God for guidance. Refreshed after a good night's sleep it was clear that my preferred path was in the healthcare field where I would gain a sense of accomplishment by utilizing my skills to help others.

As I learn more about the teachings of Jesus Christ, I increasingly come to rely on Him for guidance. I am grateful and thank Him for each and every day. I know He is always there when I need guidance and support. When my mother was ill, when my daughter was in an accident, when work is difficult, whenever life presents a challenge, it is comforting to know I don't have to face it alone. I used to think of Christianity and my relationship with Our Savior differently. In my earlier years, I had been raised to believe in the basics of Jesus Christ. He was born into this world, taught us how to live a Christian life, and paid the ultimate price by dying to save us from the consequences of sin. I never really understood why this had to happen, but was a strong believer nonetheless. Until I really studied the Word of God, my relationship with Christ seemed distant. All the teachings, readings and sermons impacted me like a great story, not real life. My eyes opened when I realized that our almighty Creator, Jesus walked the Earth just like you and me. Once I gained this perspective, the way I live my life has been transformed, from being an avid fan and spectator of the Christian faith, to someone who lives their life for Christ.

"What do you do Jim?" One of my wife's co-workers asks at their annual Christmas party. I quickly respond that I work in Information Technology planning in the Healthcare Industry. As the conversation continues, I share that I am an avid runner who has taken up swimming and biking. I share that I have been blessed with three wonderful daughters, a wonderful wife and live on a lake in White Lake, Michigan.

Later that night I recalled the conversation and thought

deeper about the question. Reflecting on that conversation I understood my life's journey has been driven by three things- my love and passion for being a Christian, my family, and being a runner. Of course, I am many other things—a father, parent, coach and professional... But my approach to how I pursue these and other things in my life have in large part been formed through the discipline I have learned from both Christianity and running.

My goal in writing this book is to share my journey and reveal insights I gained in my maturing as a Christian and as a runner... both have led me to complete confidence, happiness, and a feeling of fulfillment. The journey is what matters most and every day and moment spent pursuing the people and things you love is the ultimate reward.

Reflecting upon my life, I learned that the experiences gained through the running/Christian combination have many similarities.

The old adage "You can't get to where you are going unless you know where you are at" is a good principle to keep in mind as you begin the journey toward happiness and contentment regardless of your mission. Evaluate where you are and where you want to be athletically, professionally, artistically, spiritually or otherwise. Once you determine where you are at you can begin your growth as a Christian and a runner by starting to build a strong foundation toward your goal.   As you are exposed to new adventures, it is essential to develop a plan that will guide you through life and help you work toward and achieve your goals. As you attain milestones and progress, you will continue to raise the bar and seek out new goals and adventures. As a result of your growth, you will realize that achievement of your goals often requires hard work and sacrifice, and you will encounter many obstacles along the path. Overcoming these obstacles requires perseverance and staying the course when things don't go according to the plan. As you live your life and encounter new experiences, you will discover these new frontiers can keep you fresh in your journey. Over the long haul, you will learn that rather than reacting to daily challenges, a lifetime plan will keep you on track and allow you to continue to get the most from your adventure.

Your journey will be optimal if you keep some guiding principles in mind. First and foremost, you need a plan that is well thought-out, but flexible enough to adjust to the unforeseen situations you will encounter. You will discover you can gain strength through teamwork. Seek out resources to guide you such as companions, mentors, coaches, training plans, inspirational books, and, above all else—the written Word of God. As you strive to reach your goals, it is essential to seek leadership and expertise to provide you with the direction and support to stay on course. You will grow a great deal through intimate friendships and relationships when you learn to count on close friends as a support system. Leading by example allows you to reach out to others and contribute to growth in the groups that you participate. As family becomes a strong part of your life, you boost your faith and sport through a support system by including those closest to you. Your community will benefit when you volunteer and help those in need. Along with all the work, you will reap the biggest benefits if you learn to renew and refresh your mind and body with adequate fuel that will keep the fire of enthusiasm bright along the way.

Reaching for a lofty goal is healthy. However, you will attain a greater sense of peace in your life and closeness with God if you humbly accept success and thank our Father for providing you with the means to achieve your goals. Finally, you must remain in the present, to experience the joys and benefits of not only achieving your goals but the journey to attain them.

Chapter One

Achieving More than You Thought Was Possible

"What is impossible with man is possible with God."
Luke 18:27

I looked down at the red plywood as I positioned myself on the starting line awaiting last minute instructions from the starter. I jumped up a few times to alleviate my nervousness and then focused on the task at hand. "Get in the race and hang on as long as I could" was my strategy. I had come a long way since my first college race. My mission changed from simply being a member of the team to attempting the Eastern Michigan University (EMU),

---

varsity record in the one-mile run. The Cleveland Knights of Columbus meet was one of the major stops on the indoor track circuit during the late 1970's.

I stood in awe and silence as the PA announced the field. "In lane one, US one-mile record holder, Marty Liquori. In lane two, Olympic silver medalist from New Zealand, Dick Quax. In lane three from Kenya, former NCAA 880 yard champion, Mike Boit. In lane four from Eastern Michigan University, Jim Deren." And the list went on. I felt fortunate to have this once-in-a-lifetime opportunity to be racing against these legends—the best milers in the world. Running fast on an indoor board track was something I did not quite understand. Imagine stepping on plywood and running short straightaways and long turns that would make it nearly impossible to pass on. The only possible way to pass someone is to accelerate coming out of the turn and to sprint the next short straightway beating your competition to the turn.   My strategy was simple- avoid all of that and jump to an early lead. I hoped that the elite field would choose to run a tactical race where they followed the pacesetter for the majority of the race and then unleashed their super kicks. As the gun sounded, I focused on sprinting to the lead and then keeping an honest pace to stay there until the kicking began. As this turned out to be a tactical race for most of the field, it was an all-out effort all the way for me.

After the success I felt at the end of cross-country season, I came to indoor track, beaming with confidence and energy. In early December, the season kicked off with the annual inter-class meet, an event that was simply an early year time trial. The meet was restricted to EMU track athletes and spanned two days. As the gun sounded to signal the start of the 880-yard dash, I pushed myself into a quick lead in my heat. I was entered in the 2nd heat, meaning I was not considered one of our top eight half-milers. My goal was to run easy and try to run close to my personal best of 1:53. I passed the first 220 in 27.5 seconds, pretty close to my fastest 220, but feeling surprisingly relaxed.

I sensed my teammates on my shoulder down the backstretch and knew I had to accelerate to hold them off. "Fifty-four seconds!" I had just run a twenty-six second 220! I slowed considerably coming through 660 in 1:24—about a thirty-second lap. Hearing my split was a wake-up call as I stretched my legs around the back straightaway and around the final turn. I pumped hard to hit the tape twenty yards ahead of the next runner in a new meet record of 1:51.5. "Who is that kid?" I could hear when I jogged around the track for my cool down.

Coach Bob Parks greeted me and said "I think we just found our new anchorman... Let's see some of that against our rivals. "

I replied "Thanks, coach... I feel great."

The next day would be interesting. I had not run many one-mile races since high school and had only run one two-mile race in my life. My new-found confidence from the previous day's win encouraged me to map out a strategy to run under 4:15 in the mile; a time that would position me to be considered for varsity relays and events. As the race started, I quickly positioned myself around 4th or 5th place. We passed the quarter in sixty-three seconds and the half in 2:08. I figured that if I could hit 3:13 or better at three-quarters that my final kick could get me to my goal. As we approached three-quarters, I swung wide to begin my final ¼ mile kick. "3:12." I would need to run under sixty-three seconds. I worked hard and felt myself accelerate. Being in the lead at the gun lap was a new experience for me, so when I heard the shot, I felt a rush of adrenalin. I powered around the turn and headed for home thinking "Don't let up!!!" I crossed the tape first, knowing that I had easily beaten my goal.

My close friend and the women's track coach was the first to approach me. "Jim, do you know what you just did?"

I was perplexed... breaking 4:15 was my goal, but no big deal in the context of all of the great milers who have run for EMU.

"You just ran 4:07 flat!!!"

This is one of those moments you never forget... achieving what you thought was impossible. My time was good enough to shatter the meet record, place me 3rd on the all-time EMU list, and put me one-second away from qualifying for the Division One National Track and Field NCCA meet.

My head was spinning as I prepared for the two mile that would begin an hour later. Being a middle-distance runner, I would leave this one to the distance stars and just use it as a workout. I felt tired at the start, but soon regained my energy when I moved from the back of the pack up to the middle half-way. Fatigue was beginning to set in. "Keep it going, keep it going." With a quarter mile left, I remember feeling the pain and the slow drain of energy. All I could think was "Let's get this thing over with." I dug deep and my legs did the rest. I quickly moved into contention and as the gun sounded to signal the final lap, my body automatically shifted into another gear. My teammates cheered as I inched into the lead and edged past the leader to win in the final steps. My time of 9:03 was a good minute better than I had ever run before, let alone after finishing my third event of the meet.

As the indoor track competition season progressed, I continued to exceed my expectations by running personal bests in most of my races and relay legs. Over the next several weeks, my new-found confidence propelled me to the top ten list of U.S.

runners in the mile, half-mile, and two-mile runs. As well, it allowed me to qualify for the U.S. Nationals with a 4:06 mile, 8:48 two mile, and 1:50.2 in the 880. This also opened the door for several invites to elite invitational meets including the Cleveland K of C meet in late February.

The task at hand was to stay in contention as we raced around the board track in Cleveland. I continued to lead with an honest pace as we reached the half-mile in 2:02. Here comes the challenge. Like many runners, the third quarter of any race is the most difficult. It is the point where adrenalin runs out and fatigue begins to set in, but too early to begin the all-out final kick. As we passed laps seven and eight of the eleven-lap race, I faded for a moment and found myself moving backward in the pack. My competitive spirit failed to let me give up and encouraged me to give it my all. I held my position remembering that passing was going to be extremely difficult. As we hit lap nine, I sprinted and found myself passing two runners and moving up. Instead of tucking in, I kept the momentum going and passed two more runners entering the bell lap. I was now in second place and the kick of the elite field was in progress. As we rounded the first turn on the last lap, I trailed only one runner, Marty Liquori, the fastest miler in the United States. I moved up to his shoulder, ready to give him a run for it down the back stretch. We both all-out sprinted and were dead even as we reached the final turn. His advantage of being on the inside made me run longer and faster to move ahead. I ran high and felt the energy in my legs spring back from the boards as I sprinted to the tape, finishing second by one-tenth of a second.

Despite not winning, I was elated. This race propelled me to a new EMU varsity record and proved that I could be competitive with the best in the world. I advanced from being a walk-on extra to a varsity record holder. This taught me that dreams are possible and gave me the confidence that nothing is out of reach. Over the next two seasons, I enjoyed much success on the track: lowering the varsity record to 4:04, earning All-American twice with two fourth-place finishes, winning several relays and races and becoming team captain.   In cross-country, I earned all-district, all-conference and ran several personal-best times.

My success in collegiate running taught me several valuable lessons.   First of all, our goals may not be easily reached, but through perseverance, character and confidence we are capable of much more than we realize. More importantly I gained valuable experiences of great times and great friends that have followed me throughout my life.

****

It was a perfect winter day when I walked along the strip toward the Las Vegas Convention Center. I wore only a business suit which would not have been ideal in the sub-freezing weather back home in Michigan.

While I stood on the podium and looked out over the audience, I felt a sense of excitement. I was selected as a guest speaker for the 2012 Healthcare Information Management System Society HIMSS National Conference.   Speaking at this conference is quite an honor, as very few are selected from thousands of applicants who are experts in the field on Healthcare Information Technology (I.T.).   HIMSS is the largest and most prominent organization of Healthcare I.T. professionals in the world. Boasting a membership of over 50,000, the annual conference hosted over 37,000 professionals in 2012.   Speaking at this conference validated my credentials and career aspirations... to be the best I can be in my field and help others succeed. Based upon my colleagues' feedback I learned that my strength in speaking comes from my ability to take complex topics and make them easily understandable.

When I was young, I struggled with choosing a career path that would allow me to leverage my gifts from God.   First of all, I had no idea what those gifts were.   As I entered college and analyzed my options, I understood that I love to learn, have a knack for remembering details and enjoy interacting and helping others. I also knew that I was terrified to speak in front of groups, had no interest in mechanical things, and was not comfortable with sales. I entered college with a liberal arts major and along the way, tried to figure out my future.   During my first two years, I switched from Industrial Arts to General Business to Pre-Law and finally arrived at a field that suited me—Elementary Education.   I tried a few courses in Marketing, Accounting, and Architectural Design but became intrigued by the new up-and-coming field of Computer Science, so I pursued that as a minor.

Despite my lack of consistency in programs, I maintained A's and B's in all my classes, graduated with honors and a post-graduate scholarship; all while working multiple jobs and running track and cross-country.   I studied hard and earned good grades. Getting a job should be easy! Wrong!

Entering the job market in the late 1970's was challenging, especially if one wanted to teach and had no experience or connections. Before the days of the internet and personal computers, job searches consisted of reading the want-ads, writing inquiry letters to prospective employers, checking job postings at the universities job-placement center, and attending job fairs.   My early post-graduate days were filled with typing hundreds of cover letters, making copies of my resume, getting contacts, and receiving rejection letters.   To pay the rent, bills, and repay my student loans, I continued to work multiple jobs.   I did everything I could to earn a living including flipping burgers, washing cars, clerking midnights at a convenience store, mowing lawns, and painting houses.

The escape I got during my daily runs and weekly attendance at church helped me to keep my composure and focus. After months and months of rejections, I knew I needed to adjust my plan. I was able to land a job as a substitute teacher combined with coaching high-school track. The coaching job paid less than the cost of gas to get there, but it was something I loved to do. I was able to teach, interact, and help others... it was all there except for the money, so I worked in a restaurant at night and on weekends.

Adding the substitute teaching and coaching experience to my resume failed to land me a permanent position, so I changed directions. Knowing that the Data Processing field was in high demand, I pursued employment in the business world. I got a few interviews and finally landed my first full-time job as a computer programmer right at my alma mater, Eastern Michigan University.

My entry-level job at Eastern Michigan University provided me with the experience necessary to move into a number of industries and positions. A few years later, after landing a job at a major Detroit area hospital, I recognized and began to grow my expertise in technology and how it relates to hospitals. An underlying trait to my growth in the field came from understanding how hospitals and healthcare work and providing technical solutions to healthcare worker needs. I quickly advanced to analyst, manager, and I am currently the director of IT strategic planning for a large healthcare consulting firm. In my work, I provide insights to hospital decision-makers about which projects and processes should be their priorities. Over the years, I apply experiences and knowledge toward solving problems for hospital clients. I found that the key to effective speaking is knowledge and enthusiasm about your topic rather than memorization of it.

Run To Faith   James Deren

As I reflect, I can be quick to say how proud I am that through persistence and hard work I have earned a meaningful position. However, a closer look reveals that I had a lot of help along the way in the form of minor miracles.

When asked if you ever have experienced a miracle in your life, many people will reflect and try to recall a major unexpected event that changed their lives. A deeper look at this should reveal a series of every-day miracle events that can span a lifetime. As I reflected, it dawned on me that many of the challenges I endured over the years steered me in the direction that led to my position today. Working multiple jobs, running, and barely paying the rent taught me to set my priorities. The hours and years I spent trying to land a job taught me patience. Studying and understanding my customers' needs helped me gain the expertise needed to speak in front of crowds. Difficult work situations helped me to appreciate my comfort and desire to work in the healthcare industry. An education degree and coaching experience helped me gain an appreciation for teaching and mentoring others.

I realized that the events of my life and eventual outcomes were set up by God through His plan for me. As new challenges are presented, I have gained inner peace and strength knowing that this is more than bad luck or coincidence. It is a part of God's plan. I firmly believe that God want's what is best for each of us and these worldly events and situations are how He uses this world to draw us nearer to Him. God does not ignore our desires and prayers, but may answer them in ways we don't expect. What I had asked for many years ago was a purposeful life where I could use my talents. I wanted to teach, interact with others, help others and continue to learn. I realize now that all of these have been provided along with the gift of Eternal happiness.

Pursuing your goals takes perseverance, consistency, and patience.   Whether it is running, career, relationships or spirituality, things don't always go as planned. The key to fulfillment is to ensure that your goals are achievable yet challenging.   Fulfillment of goals is most likely accompanied by a brief period of rest and satisfaction and then moving on to a higher standard.   Sticking it out through hard times and many disappointments are often necessary to experience a significant breakthrough.

Knowing that God has your back will give you great comfort through the assurance that He may not provide everything you want, but will provide what you need. Negative energy can be minimized if we keep in mind that no matter what the outcome of our requests to God, He will provide us with the only goal that really matters… eternal life with Him.

Chapter Two

I'm Already There

"The Kingdom of God is in the midst of you." Luke 17:21

The alarm was set to ring at five-thirty in the morning. However, I woke a few minutes before and made my way out of bed. I could feel the warmness in the air when I walked by the thermometer in the dining room that already registered seventy-nine degrees. As sure as it is cold in Michigan in January, it is always hot on the 4th of July. I made the coffee and woke my wife and two daughters. July 4th is a tradition in our household of heading to Frankenmuth for the "Volklaufe" road race. To stay on schedule, we planned to leave at six in the morning, pick up my oldest daughter, her husband, friend and their dogs; then make the one-hour ride up US-23 to Frankenmuth, Michigan in ample time to pick up our numbers, t-shirts and do some jogging.

The city of Frankenmuth has been a destination of Michigan travelers for many years. It is a small, friendly community located in Mid-Michigan and known for its' Bavarian flavor. This rural farming community is known year-round for the famous Zehnder Chicken Dinners, the Bavarian Restaurant and Bakery, The Frankenmuth Brewery, several crafts and antique shops and the worlds' largest indoor Christmas display. On the fourth of July, however, it is host to one of the countries' oldest road races, the "Volklaufe", that offers a 20K, 10K, 5K run and walk, and one mile fun run.

The word "Volkslaufe" is German for the "People's Race" and is fitting as this event is targeted to the local residents of the area. In the thirty-plus years that the event has existed, it has been marked by July 3rd fireworks; morning pancake breakfast; German polka music; smell of chicken barbeque dinners and beer tent aromas. The starting cannon blast of the first event and the prized German beer steins awarded to age-group winners and filled with beer, of course.

The Frankenmuth Chamber of Commerce has retained the local flavor of the runs using volunteers, incorporating the city and local farming areas on the course and keeping entry fees lower than most other runs. Still, the number of participants continues to hover in the thousands.

The color of the morning sky was spectacular, but also an indication of the ensuing heat that would challenge the runners. As we arrived at Heritage Park, we quickly encountered many of our friends as fellow runners and race volunteers. My wife Deb, daughters Rose and Renee, son-in-law Greg, and his friend Erich were all entered in the 10K which began at seven-fifty in the morning. I had been putting in extra speed work and chose the 5K as my best chance for a beer stein award. My daughter Rachel agreed to take pictures, watch the dogs, cheer for us and jump into the 5K walk. I chatted with friends and stood on the sidelines as the cannon sounded to signify the start of the 10K run. Rachel and I took a shortcut and hurried across the park with the hope of finding a good spot to watch the runners head out onto the course. We looked through the crowd of a thousand runners and picked out our family and friends offering words of encouragement. A few minutes later the 20K race began and although our family was not participating, we looked for and encouraged not only our friends but all of the runners as they headed into town in the scorching heat.

After the last runners had passed, there were a few minutes of eerie silence that was quickly broken by the sight of the 10K leaders returning. Near the front of the pack, we picked out Debbie, who had built a large lead as the first masters' woman. A few minutes later we cheered for Rose, Renee, Greg, and Erich as well as other friends as they made their way to the finish.

Soon after, I prepared to warm-up and make my way to the start of the 5K which began at nine o'clock. I pinned on my number and convinced Rachel to participate by accompanying me in the 5K. Looking up at the crowd of runners made me reminisce about past years experiences. Almost thirty-five years ago, I stood on the same spot with a similar goal of earning an age-group award in the 20K race. As a twenty-five-year-old, I completed my senior year as a distance runner at Eastern Michigan University, where I had earned two All-American medals and captured the varsity records in the one mile distance medley, and sprint medley relays. Back then, my plan was to run five-minute miles for as long as possible, however in 1977, just as today, the ever present heat was sure to have an impact on the times. Ten and twenty years later, I toed the line with the slightly slower but a similar goal of being competitive. As the years passed, my pace and endurance had slowed, but the goal of earning a top-three age-group spot was still something I aimed for.

The past two years had mixed results. My training was going well, but slightly hampered by the nagging injuries that come with age. I finished 4th in my age group in the 10K, missing the prizes by less than ten seconds both times. To prove I still had the competitive nature in me, I jumped in the 5K last year and finished 2nd.   In preparation for this year's race, I added intervals and tempo runs to my weekly routine. It seemed to be working since I was the overall winner of a local 10K earlier in the year.

As the starting time neared, it was evident this year would be different. About a month prior to the race, I was on a recovery run that started with extreme tightness in my left hamstring. While I worked through the run, the tightness turned to numbness and weakness. I struggled home hoping a few days of rest would alleviate the pain. For a couple of weeks, I tested the leg with no improvement, in fact, the weakness became more apparent and began to affect my walking. As this years' 5K was nearing, I finally realized that my body was unable to run. My depression and self-pity were quickly erased as my daughter Rachel enthusiastically encouraged me to participate by walking the route.

I made my way to the back of the runners where other walkers assemble for the event. I quickly noticed that the sights and sounds were very different than the tense excitement I had become accustomed to in past years near the front lines. Participants around us were much more at ease as they talked, joked, wore headphones, and talked on iPhones. As the gun sounded, we began our trek through the streets of Frankenmuth.

Walking the course, this year introduced me to many new

experiences. Despite running this route for the past thirty years, I had never noticed a river and park that line the left side of the course.   Nor had I noticed the number of families who had set up water stations and signs in their front yards. At the one-mile mark was a dance group followed a few yards later by a polka band.   The covered bridge at mile two was slightly uphill and the three-mile aid station was manned by Bavarian-clad volunteers.

When I neared the finish line, I noticed the crowd cheering for all the participants. To the right was my family offering words of encouragement.   At that point, I was overcome with an intense feeling of satisfaction.   For forty years, running races was about training consistently and then pushing myself to the max.   This feeling was very different.   Walking in the sunshine with my daughter, hearing the crowd support, and being with my family made me feel fortunate of who I was and where I was.   I realized that striving to accomplish my goals would always leave me setting a new goal and wanting more. I realized in the quest to achieve what I wanted most out of running was that I had already achieved it, just by participating.

As we grow and mature, we find the process of setting incremental goals will give each of us a higher probability of success than reaching for the stars immediately.   Fulfilling our dreams is often a long process that takes patience and perseverance.

When I was a freshman in high school, I began my lifelong journey as a runner by establishing some goals.   First, it was to earn my varsity letter, then to run a mile in 4:30. As I achieved each goal, I continued to raise the bar—to run for a college team, then to make the varsity and finally to break the varsity record and earn All-American status. More importantly, I understood that falling short of a goal can be rewarding. In my quest to break 4 minutes in the mile, I fell short, however, gained numerous positive experiences and memories that have become a part of who I am.

Setting appropriate goals and striving to achieve them is essential for a happy and fulfilling life. To get the most out of your pursuits, the goals that you set should be both attainable and challenging. The standards you set for yourself help to define who you are; therefore it is important your goals are personal and not someone else's expectation. "Now that I have a goal what is my plan to get there?" The goal of completing the Boston Marathon may start with being able to run one mile, five miles, ten miles and more along the way. If your goal is to finish a triathlon, start your own company, raise your children to be successful, or lose five pounds, it needs to come from a strong desire within.

Keep in mind results matter less than your growth as an individual through the experiences, insights and disciplines you gain along the way.   Similarly, your goal of contentment and eternal peace with Jesus Christ requires a roadmap that includes incremental milestones along the way. Praying, studying the Bible, fellowship with others and performing acts of kindness are some of the training techniques that will transform you into the Christian person you long to be.   In striving to raise successful children, take the time to enjoy teaching your children to read, playing games with them and cheering for them in school activities. Remember the ten-mile trail training run on the perfect fall day in the park where you felt like you could run forever. Remember how you ran through the pain on a character-building run in the ten-degree snowstorm. When pursuing your dreams, getting there is half the fun.

Chapter Three

In the Beginning

"An intelligent heart acquires knowledge, and the ears of a wise man seek knowledge." Proverbs 18:15

Is he okay? I heard from the crowd. "Just keep coming," I thought to myself while I awaited my teammate in preparation for beginning my leg of the mile relay. A few moments ago I was ecstatic as our third runner built a commanding lead on the backstretch. My thoughts quickly changed from assurance that I could hold off my competitors to "I really have to run hard." As my classmate Dave staggered toward the line, I felt both compassion for his effort and anger at him for putting me in this predicament. It was track and field day in junior high and the final event, the mile relay was coming to a close. I grabbed the baton, put my head down, and started to run.

"Here's the pitch—it's a line shot, base hit, Kaline scores and the Tigers have won their first pennant since 1968." 1968 was a great time to be a fourteen-year-old kid in Detroit. It was a simple time and we had fun doing things that kids today would have trouble relating to. Advancements in technology, since I was a child, have changed the way the kids of today use their time. Before video games, smart phones, texting, and the internet, entertainment was driven by personal interaction and creativity. Baseball was the big sport and the Tigers were followed by everyone. Interacting with total strangers was easy… because all you had to ask was "How are the Tigers doing?" Tiger Stadium was an exciting place to take in a game and we did a lot of that. As a kid, you could save a few Ball-Park Frank hot dog wrappers and redeem them for a ticket to sit in the bleachers. At the park, on your front porch, at the beach, on the bus… everywhere you went, you could hear the voice of Ernie Harwell calling the game on the radio.

The city of Detroit was in transition and trying to forget the devastating events of 1967—the year of the riots in Detroit and the year the Tigers lost the pennant on the final day of the season.

Gasoline was thirty-four cents a gallon. You could buy a used car for $500, teenagers and coeds frequented peace-fests and sit-ins and listened to the music of the Beatles, Rolling Stones, Four Tops and the Doors. While fast food generally meant TV dinners, 1968 introduced us to the Big Mac and the first automatic teller machines. Our summertime wardrobe looked straight out of the

Sandlot movie and consisted of several white t-shirts and Keds tennis shoes. Color TV was reserved for the upper-class and everyone had a transistor AM radio. Many kids were in touch with politics as most remembered the television broadcast of the assassination of President John F. Kennedy just five years prior. Political leaders Robert Kennedy and Martin Luther King Jr. had been shot and killed. The Vietnam War was the lead story on TV News and many of us had relatives or neighbors who were drafted and served our country.

The distraction from electronic devices did not exist. We spent most of our time outdoors, interacting with and talking face-to-face with our friends. From the time we woke up until we got home at night, we were attached to our bikes. During the summer, we spent the day playing games such as baseball, basketball, ping pong, tag, and capture the flag. After a fifteen cent Cherry Coke at Mary's store and fine reading of the latest Superman comic book, we rested by watching TV shows like the Addams Family and Gilligan's Island.

I attended 1st through 8th in a Parochial School. I entered Lessenger Junior High School for 9th grade. The amount of freedom at a public school was a dramatically different than the highly structured environment provided by the nuns who had been our teachers through 8th grade. The most popular event in 9th grade was gym class "Dodgeball". There were two ways of being eliminated, either you caught someone's throw or hit someone without them catching the ball. The only unwritten rule was that you never wanted to catch one of the big kid's throws or you had to deal with after-hours retribution.

Ninth grade is the age that contains an extremely wide variation in a child's physical development. Students ranged from six foot three inches tall and two hundred pounds to five foot three inches in height and one hundred pounds. Inevitably the game seemed to always end tragically, with five big kids heaving a ball from twenty feet at the smallest kid in the class.

In 1968, there were few middle-school sports teams. Girls had the limited choice of tennis, field hockey or softball, and the boy's sports options included baseball, basketball, football, track, and swimming. Despite a lack of organized sports most kids ran, jumped, biked, swam, and played baseball, football, and basketball in frequent pick-up games.

Although I loved to run and race my friends, I didn't officially run for time until junior high school. The big event of the year was "track and field day" which was held on the last day of the school year. The event wasn't properly named as the events consisted of only a few events – the longest baseball throw, 100-yard dash, and what was thought to be the distance race—the "mile relay". The winning class was awarded a large trophy that was displayed in the school hallway display case.

Each homeroom selected four runners who would each run about a quarter mile around a drawn up path in the park across the street. Our class decided that the first four finishers in our gym class timed mile run would be the representatives.

On a cool spring morning our gym class, dressed in our white shorts, Keds, and white t-shirt with the blue letters "Lessenger" written across the chest, assembled for the mile run. At that point, we had no idea how far a mile was—we just knew it was a long way. We were instructed to run along the white chalk line through the nearby valley and onto the path until we saw the gym teachers.

The biggest kids lined up in front, certain that they would

dominate the run. As the gun sounded, they bolted out quickly and took the lead. I hung back with a few of my classmates for a while, but suddenly had this feeling of lightness and made my move upward through the pack. After a few minutes, I caught the leaders who were fading quickly. I moved into the lead as I spotted the gym teachers in the distance. It seemed that we had not run very long and I was convinced that once we reached them we would need to turn around and run back to the start. To my surprise, I reached them first and the mile was over. My time was 5:42.

Earning a spot on the mile relay team transformed me quickly from a regular kid to a school celebrity. In the week before the final event, I listened to advice and coaching from most of my classmates about how to run the race. Our team was thought to be underdogs to a few other classes of bigger kids, who up until then had dominated all athletic events.

Our fifth runner from the gym class mile run was the designated coach and decided the lineup. My friend Rick, who had finished second, would run leadoff and I would run anchor. "Hold back and pace yourself. A quarter mile is a long way and you don't want to die" were his words of wisdom. As the starting gun sounded, I for the first time—and many times in later years got the nervous feeling in my stomach that I have come to know well. Rick paid no attention to the coaching and jumped out into the lead. My classmates stood around the first turn motioning for him to slow down—but he just kept going and going. His lead built from five to ten to twenty yards as he entered the home straightaway. The school seemed to have picked us as their favorites—hoping we would unseat the big tough kids as the champions.

Our next runner was Fred, a red-haired kid who was also the class clown. Fred held his own and maintained most of the lead.

However the 2nd and 3rd place team stormed back to make it a three-team race. Our third runner was Dave, a confident kid who was better than average at school and sports. Dave was determined to show off his athleticism and sprinted the first one hundred yards gaining back the thirty-yard lead. Dave settled into a nice pace and kept his long lead around the far side of the track. As I stood there, I prayed that he would continue to keep the lead so that I would be in a position to bring home a win. As Dave came around the final turn, the inevitable happened. He began to tighten up and slowed quickly. The more he tried to power to the finish the slower he got. That was the first time I was introduced to the term "The Bear jumped on his back". He ran toward me like he was carrying a five-hundred-pound bear on his back—and quickly not only lost the lead, but fell further and further back to second, third, and then fourth place.

I looked at my competition and saw that Duane Finn, the fastest kid in school who had previously won the 100-yard dash was running anchor for the big guys. My heart raced and my nerves screamed. When I got the baton, I felt anxious and energetic and decide that the only shot of winning was to go out quickly, pick it up and see what I had left. I sprinted around the first turn and quickly found myself caught up to the second and third place teams. I looked up and saw Duane had extended the lead to what seemed like an insurmountable distance. I passed the other runners and moved into second, I felt a rush of adrenalin through my legs. I lifted my legs and began to sprint as hard as I could. I was making up ground but not sure if there was enough room left to catch him. I entered the last straightaway and I was still twenty yards behind. I summoned all my strength and forgot about the crowd, the noise, or any fatigue, only thinking about turning my legs over faster. He was getting closer and closer when I saw the finish line tape.   With a final surge, I lunged toward the line and overtook him with two steps left to win my first race and claim the track and field day championship for my class.

I was quickly congratulated by my team and told my split was sixty seconds flat. I wasn't sure what that meant, but knew that it was a feeling I wanted to experience again.

****

You hit it, now you get it. The mood at the playground changed from elation to frustration as we just lost our only baseball. Just a few seconds ago I was beaming with elation as I rounded the bases. I crushed the pitch sending it over the eight-foot wall that separated our makeshift baseball field with the convent backyard of the nuns who taught us at school. The scene mirrored that of the movie the Sandlot where stories had been told for generations about what was behind the wall. "There was a kid a few years ago who went in there and never came back. We think they have a big dog they use to attack intruders."

"I hear the nuns can't ever remove their habits—even when they sleep." As the years passed, the stories became more outrageous. "A kid went in there a few years ago and was forced to say two-thousand Our Fathers before they let him go." Despite all these stories, I knew the group was looking to me to retrieve the ball so we could return to our game. I sized up the situation and devised my plan. I would go around the back of the yard where there was a wooden gate that would give me a way to climb over the wall. I jumped on the first rung and pulled myself to the top. "Do you see it?" they asked from below. The trees obstructed my view and I couldn't see much of the yard. I lifted myself over and jumped to the ground inside the fortress. The landing was far from graceful as I fell flat on my face. I looked up, startled by a voice. "Looking for this?" I gasped for air and I found myself sweating profusely, afraid to move. Sister Mary Rose was standing over me holding the ball. "Are you okay? "she asked. "If you wanted the ball why didn't you come to the door and ask?" I was speechless but relieved. I looked around and was shocked to see the normalcy of the yard and my surroundings. I quickly recognized a couple of my teachers playing a game of cards and others reading. I hadn't planned my escape, which became unnecessary as the Sister Mary Rose led me through the house. I passed through a few rooms that included a sitting area with a TV, a kitchen, and library. "Why don't you rest for a second? Let me get you a few cookies and something to drink." Sister said in a caring and soft voice. We sat at the table and chatted about baseball, school, and our families. "This is all right." I thought to myself. I realized that we had been unfair to the nuns, judging them on undocumented and outrageous made-up stories.

After my twenty-minute rest, I walked out the front door, baseball in hand, wondering why anyone would be afraid of the hospitable nuns. "What happened? Did they hurt you?" my friends inquired when I returned to the ball field.

"Almost, they made me sit in the kitchen and were going to call my parents but when they looked away I bolted for the door and escaped."

"Wow, how cool!" My secret was safe.

Long before I was able to establish a religious identity, I was baptized into our church, much like all of my siblings and generations before them. I was fortunate to have parents who were believers in a traditional religious upbringing and our faith and family life revolved around these principals.   My introduction to Christianity began at an early age when my mother taught my brothers, sisters and me to pray and honor God. My father was a hard-working man who worked six days a week, ten hours a day, for as long as I can remember. My mother stayed at home and cooked, cleaned and cared for us six children with few of the modern conveniences that we expect and take for granted today. Conveniences such as microwave ovens, wrinkle free clothes, precooked meals, and disposable diapers had not been invented. The typical family relied upon a single car and single black and white television. Both parents were actively involved in the St. Peter and Paul parish in the Altar Society, Dads' Club and as choir members. We lived in a middle-class neighborhood in Detroit with most of our aunts, uncles and cousins less than a mile away.

The houses and yards were small in the clean, friendly, westside of Detroit neighborhood, but it was all we needed. Every street was full of kids who were always outside playing; many of whom were my classmates at Saint Peter and Paul School.

My first recollection of going to school was in August of 1960 as I was getting ready for first grade at the age of six. My mother took my brother, my two oldest sisters, and I to the clothes store on Warren Avenue to get fitted for our school uniforms. Warren Avenue, which was six houses down the street from my home, was the hub of activity in the neighborhood. On the corner was a drugstore that we frequented and further down the way a dime store, a couple bakeries, a butcher shop, fresh fruit market and grocery store. The environment was quite a contrast to current times where the majority of neighborhoods consist of the sameness of popular chains such as 7-11 stores, McDonalds, Walgreens, ACE Hardware, and Dairy Queen. Back then, communities were served by our neighbors and family-run businesses such as Joe's Hardware, Stromboli Pizzeria, and the Warrendale Bakery. At the clothing store, I was promptly measured and came away with three blue shirts, two pairs of navy slacks, and a couple blue clip-on ties. This ritual continued for the next eight years. I did not learn to tie a tie until I was fourteen.

The first time I entered the school, I was frightened by my

first-grade teacher, Sister Mary Elizabeth, the large woman dressed in black and white from head to toe. Although the clothing has changed over the years, I am still fearful when I see a nun. That feeling dominated the early years of my upbringing as "Instilling the Fear of The Lord" seemed to be the ongoing theme of my childhood. The parochial school we attended was characterized by countless rules and regulations. We would line up to go to school, line up to go to the bathroom, line up to go to church and line up to go home. Traversing through the school meant walking in line on the third tile from the wall. Being one of the shorter kids in class, since we were lined up by height, I was always near the front. Every nun was issued a weapon such as a steel ruler or paddle that could be used to discipline kids at their discretion. If kids were particularly unruly, Father Redwig was called in to handle things. The last thing you wanted to happen was for the nuns to call your parents, as they teamed together to inflict punishment.

Every day began with lining up and walking single file on the third square to the church for mass. Following the mass was Religion class where we learned about Christianity and prepared for our first Confession, Communion, and Confirmation. We didn't always agree with or understand the lessons immediately, however, many of the concepts came clear and stuck with me later in life. Others were hard to grasp and we quietly questioned their validity. It was a culture that didn't question authority or the concepts that were taught. Whether the teachers, parents or other adults directed us, the answer to the question "Why?" was always "because I said so"... end of discussion. Despite some skepticism, this environment helped me to establish an appreciation for Jesus and the gifts He has provided to us. We grew up with good morals and the desire to do the right thing—out of respect and a bit of fear of authority that included our parents, teachers, elders and our Lord. We knew we should be accountable for our actions and were driven to earn the respect of those around us.

My early perspective on going to church was that of sacrifice. The church building was a giant structure filled with statues, stained glass, candles, the altar and a large crucifix of Jesus facing us from behind the altar.   We were often reminded to be quiet and pay attention—however paying attention was difficult in that the service was conducted in Latin—a language very few ten-year-olds have mastered. The choir was accompanied by a loud organ that often played solemn hymns that put us into a sleepy trance. The best I could guess the church service was a type of penance and if we stuck it out we would be spiritually rewarded.

Preparing for weekly confession was a challenge. Our teacher would lead us in "an examination of conscience" where she would read a list of sins from which we would choose to confess to the priest.   A ten-year-olds' sins consisted of the usual things, fighting with my sister, using swear words and disobeying my parents. Pretty much every confession consisted of the usual script of saying that I swore ten times, fought with my sister twice, disobeyed my parents three times and had evil thoughts twice. After saying ten Hail Mary's and ten Our Fathers I was good to go until next time.

Over time, we discovered ways to liven up the daily school routine. Joining the choir was good to get us out of religion class once a week. We volunteered to clean the school so that we could get out of class whenever possible. Joining the Safety Patrol enabled us to get a few extra minutes each day outside of the classroom before and after school; as well as earning a trip to a Tiger ball game on a school day in the spring.

These early years set the stage for the next thirty years where I aspired to be a good person by attending mass, going to confession and saying ten Hail Mary's and ten Our Fathers whenever necessary. I learned accountability for my actions and gained a sense of obligation to do the right thing when given a choice. There were many occasions where I learned that overcoming challenges and difficult moments provided a better sense of accomplishment than if everything came easily.

Learning and growing is a lifelong activity. As we absorb more information, we continue to grow intellectually and socially. We are often taught to comply with doctrines and rules without question. However, we are more apt to get the most out of life by posing questions in a quest to understand why things are the way, they are. As we grow in our walk of faith, Jesus instructed us to be obedient to His Word, however also challenged us to pursue truth and an understanding of His teachings. Jesus instructs us… *"Ask, and it will be given to you; seek, and you will find; knock, and it will be opened to you. For everyone who asks receives, and the one who seeks finds, and to the one who knocks it will be opened." Matthew 7:7-8*

The early years of life are characterized by absorption of new information and compliance with the things we are told, but as we mature, we seek to understand these things to embrace and appreciate them. Our Father did not create us simply to follow the rules but to get to know Him and establish a personal relationship based on His grace, faith and love.

Chapter Four

Growing Up

"Then I saw and considered it; I looked and received instruction." *Proverbs 24:32*

Chucka, chucka, chucka... To this day, I still remember the sound of digging my two-inch spikes into the cinder tracks that were a mainstay of my high school track memories. When I rounded the straightaway toward the gun lap, I couldn't get that sound out of my head. I looked ahead and noticed in the distance a blue McKenzie high school jersey about thirty yards ahead and the green jersey of my teammate about twenty yards ahead of him. I was pleasantly surprised by the amount of energy I had as I was coming close to completing the 3rd lap in my first-ever high-school mile race. Like most high-schoolers, the first quarter mile was no problem. I didn't have much of a strategy other than just running the first lap and seeing where I was at. I heard the split of sixty-seven seconds when I completed the first lap but had no idea what that meant. I was tucked back in 7th or 8th place with little distance between the top eight runners in the race. My plan at that point was to keep moving and focus on the runner directly ahead of me. I remained comfortable, feeling like I was continuing the same pace and knowing that I needed to save my energy for what remained ahead of me. We approached the half-way point, and I noticed the top four runners beginning to open a gap between themselves and the rest of us. "Why are they speeding up?" I thought to myself. We passed the half-mile mark. I heard the time of 2:25. I did the math quickly and although my pace felt constant, my time told me I had run that lap ten to eleven seconds slower than the first. No wonder I was falling behind.

My instinct told me to get out of my comfort zone and see if I could make up some of the gap. When I approached the far side of the track, I moved past a couple of runners into 5th place. I continued to drive my legs without breaking into a sprint; thinking "Go fast but save something for the end."

Around the last curve, I approached the 4th and 3rd place runners and worked my way past them as the gun sounded to signify the final lap. 3:35... 3:36... I had run that lap in seventy seconds—much better. I held my own around the curve and as we hit the backstretch, I felt myself accelerate. The blue jersey was getting closer and by the time we reached the final turn, I was even with the McKenzie high school runner. The crowd cheered loudly for their runner to pick up the pace. When I came off the turn, he faded and I turned my attention to my teammate who had a ten yard lead. I dug deep and continued to close and just ran out of room, crossing the finish line second in a time of 4:41. I felt good about the sixty-five-second last lap but also felt I had a lot of room for improvement.

After the run, I savored the feeling of knowing I had given it my best. It was a different feeling than I had ever experienced before-tired and having felt pain but also joy. This would be a feeling I would come to know and enjoy over the next forty to fifty years of running and racing.

Attending high school in the early 1970's has a lot of similarities to what kids experience today. It's a time in your life when there is a strong sense of wanting to belong to a group, gaining acceptance by peers and establishing your identity. At Cody High School in Southwest Detroit, it was a particular challenge as the enrollment for 10th, 11th, and 12th grades stood at over two thousand students. The groups that were easily identifiable were the gang types, the burn-outs, the intellectuals, the car geeks, band members, the athletes and the rest. Even if you didn't identify with the larger groups, it was advisable to belong to a circle of friends or risk being forgotten in the crowd. During the Fall and Winter of my first year, I mostly just went to school and hung out with the friends I had made in grade school. Longing to grow my circle of friends and establish an identity, I weighed my options and decided to pursue an extra-curricular sports activity. This was something I enjoyed, plus I could establish myself as an athlete.

Cody High School is a member of Detroit Public Schools, a league of twenty-four schools that span the city of Detroit. In the 1970's the Public School League, PSL, boasted several outstanding athletes including future MLB, NBA and NFL stars and a number of world-class track athletes. I had my work cut out for me as the high school athletic skill level was several rungs higher than my intimate group of friends from grade school and junior high. In the 1970's, students had fewer sports program choices. There were no soccer moms, mini-vans, SUVs, or travel leagues. The sports of soccer, lacrosse, hockey, equestrian, and gymnastics were non-existent at any high school. Before Title IX, women's sports were limited to field hockey, tennis, swimming and volleyball.   After getting cut from basketball and baseball tryouts, I became dejected. However I also became more determined than ever to discover my talent and belong to a team. My memory of running in junior high school inspired me to try track and field.

Each day at Cody High school started with homeroom where the teacher took attendance and students listened to the daily announcements over the public address system. One early spring morning, an announcement caught my attention… "anyone interested in running track should report to the gym at four o'clock."

When I entered the gym, my stomach was a little queasy. I was clearly out of my comfort zone and away from the circle of friends I had made over the past several years. I was longing to gain acceptance from my fellow students, but anxious about fitting in. Pursuing this goal enlightened me with one of life's early lessons… the more I wanted something… the more anxious I would get. I looked around the gym, recognizing a number of faces I had seen before, but no one I had spent any time with. I was somewhat relieved since I realized a large number of 1st year students were a part of the contingent and were most likely thinking the same thing.

As Coach Knox rounded up the runners, I silently questioned his level of expertise and credentials for coaching track. He seemed old—at least forty—and was overweight, not the picture of someone I thought could provide expertise about the activity of running. He explained how he expected runners to attend all practices, support each other at meets, and give a good effort in their events. He also explained that you needed to score ten points to earn your Varsity letter. Cody High School had been a track power in the early 1960's but was going through some lean years, not having won a meet in three years. I think the coach was happy to see the large contingent of hopeful new runners. Coach explained each event and encouraged us to align ourselves in areas we were interested in. I knew I had limited choices if I wanted to be successful and achieve my goal of earning a Varsity letter. I couldn't hurdle, high jump, pole vault, throw weight or sprint, but my memory of junior high school gave me confidence that I could run distance events.

It didn't take long to experience the camaraderie of high school distance running. First-year runners learned quickly that distance running required more work, dedication, and time than sprinting or field events. After the first few weeks of running every day and logging several miles, I understood how difficult distance running is as I was constantly tired and sore. I thought if I was talented at any of the other sports I had considered, I would be doing those instead. I recalled the fun associated with playing baseball or basketball. I had always associated jumping in the pool or lake with having fun. At this point, track was hard work rather than the fun I had imagined when I signed up. My theory that other runners were here because they wanted to participate but were not especially good at other sports was confirmed after learning most of the distance running candidates had been cut from other sports or shifted over from sprinting or field events to make the team. As the commitment and dedication to the sport became apparent, several of those who had come out for track realized they lacked the passion needed to persevere as a distance runner and subsequently quit the team; leaving us die-hards to fill the distance running spots.

After two weeks of practice, I made quite an impression on the coach and teammates by finishing at or near the front of all workouts. The upperclassmen quickly accepted me in their circle of friends. On a warm-up run, Joe Corona, a senior co-captain, talked about the past cross-country season and wondered why I didn't join the team last fall. I was puzzled but recalled seeing students running in the fall and thinking at the time that it was odd. Detroit in the early 1970's had no road races, no running clubs, and few runners trained year round. The group abruptly came to a stop when I explained that I had never heard of cross-country and didn't know there was such as sport.

During that track season, I grew from someone who runs into a runner. I became accustomed to running intervals on a path around the football field that was about a quarter mile in length; distance runs of up to five miles; and races on cinder tracks in the city of Detroit. At each dual meet during my first season, I consistently ran the mile and a leg on the mile relay. My best time for the mile, that year was 4:38—good enough for me to achieve my goal of earning my Varsity letter.

The next fall, I joined the cross-country team. I was amazed this sport existed and that I had missed it. The high school team was middle-of-the-pack in our league and ranked much lower when we competed at Regionals or Invites. In the early 1970's, high school distance was two and a half miles. The majority of races were in Rouge Park, which was virtually a home course, being a mile from my school and home. I was delighted the cross-country course used by the high school was the same course on which I had run my junior high timed mile. This course was ideally suited for runners and spectators alike. Dual meets were conducted like invites, with multiple teams from several leagues running together and being sorted out in the results to determine the winner. This format provided us the opportunity to watch races before and after ours, giving us a glimpse of the level of talent in our area. Two city runners, Nick Ellis, and Amos Brown, stood out as being much faster than the rest of runners in the league. To watch them grow sizeable leads and win all of their races by wide margins was inspiring. Over the years Nick, who later became a teammate of mine at Eastern Michigan University, continued to improve and finished high school with a state record of 8:58 for two miles. Amos excelled in cross country and ran 4:14 as a high school miler.

I continued to meet more area runners and my perspective of the world grew. I became more aware of the environment and lifestyles around me. I learned about the economic differences of teenagers who I competed against. I was surprised that many suburban schools had the means to provide their runners with a number of amenities our team had never thought about; including new shoes and spikes, warm-ups, all-weather tracks, athletic trainers and year-round programs.

High school track and cross-country was instrumental in growing friendships and making acquaintances, from the small group of friends that I had grown up with, to an ever-expanding group of friends who shared the strong running bond. The time my fellow distance runners and I spent together included hours of sharing stories, dreams, and goals. As we grew, we collectively learned what teamwork was all about. My world broadened to include teammates who, despite our various backgrounds, shared the common trait of running for Cody High School. I was exposed to a variety of lifestyles, both poor and wealthy. I learned about the challenges my teammates Mike and Rick dealt with—coming from single-parent homes. I saw the ugly side of racism, racial slurs and prejudice that my friends Tony and James were exposed to on a daily basis. This was just the beginning of my interaction with people who for social, economic and cultural differences could share the bond of friendship through a common passion.

During my junior and senior year, I continued to show steady progress in my running. My confidence grew and I improved my performances. My teammates and I pushed and supported one another completing extra workouts and running all year long. Our goal of being the best we could was realized during my senior year with our second-place finish out of twenty-four schools in the city-wide cross-country meet. My final high school race, the Detroit Public School League, meet ended with a second-place all-city achievement and a personal best mile of 4:30. After that I didn't think much about competing, I just knew I was a runner for life; more importantly, realizing I had made several lifetime friends.

****

Sitting in the woods, I noticed the beauty of the lake and trees surrounding the wooded area just north of Port Huron on the banks of Lake Huron. I was attending a weekend camp sponsored by our church and school's teen club. A long-haired man in his twenties was playing the Beatles "My Sweet Lord" on his guitar during the outdoor church service. The setting was a far cry from the traditional organ music that echoed during Sunday mass at St. Peter and Paul Church. It was unique to see approximately one hundred teenagers fully engaged in the experience, knowing this counted as fulfillment of our weekly mass obligation. This worship service was very different from the traditional Sunday morning ritual that I was accustomed to and made me feel a bit uncomfortable, but was inspiring nonetheless. The experience of the non-traditional worship service on this summer morning left a large impact on my thoughts about Christianity.   It inspired me to think differently when I noticed my motives slowly changed away from being driven by a sense of fear and obligation. I shifted to a motivational force sincerely thanking and praising God for the gift of my life. I gained a new perspective about my spiritual journey and the purpose of my life as a result of my time at that camp. Those experiences helped me pursue relationships with others based upon friendship rather than personal gain and the question "what can you do for me?" The challenges of high school became easier to deal with when I recognized and was drawn toward those who had similar insights about Christianity. I was encouraged by what I learned and became supportive of others with troubles or needs that I could help address. I learned that seeking out friendship and strong, faithful relationships provided me with a sense of joy toward helping others

Entering a Detroit public high school meant a big lifestyle change that accompanied the graduation from a parochial grade school. Like my childhood friends, our spiritual transition included attending a weekly, teen club meeting for religious instruction. Gone was the structure that came from the grade-school teaching nuns. It was replaced by young, energetic, non-clerical leaders teaching us through real-world activities including movies, sporting events, volunteer projects and religious retreats. We could suddenly relate to our instructors as the messages we learned growing up were applied to real life experiences.

Those experiences included exposure to unfamiliar cultures and people whose lifestyle and environment were very different than mine. Especially impactful were outings to the poverty stricken areas of Detroit in which I saw the neediness of many people in our world. Outings to the inner city of Detroit included feeding the hungry, repairing building, and cleaning yards as well as food and clothing drives. The fundraising and work we performed helped me realize that I can make a difference.

High school is a time where young adults are exposed to new experiences that include temptations and unethical behaviors such as underage drinking, drugs, and sex. I learned that approaching troublesome situations with a Christian heart made it easier to recognize right from wrong and helped me to deal with things positively. Certain times, however, dealing with peer group pressure became more intense and difficult to deal with. It took strength and a strong will to decline invitations to popular parties where drinking and drugs were prevalent. During summer, the religious teen group ended and I felt a void since I was left with the traditional Sunday service as my primary source of religious inspiration. Without the consistent support of the leaders and friends I made at the retreat, I had trouble sustaining my enthusiasm for seeking a life that was spiritually relevant at all times. By the time I entered my later high school years, the sameness of the Sunday mass ritual made the repetitive prayers and songs little more than a memorization of words.

Despite the lack of excitement and enthusiasm I felt during the weekly Sunday ritual, I developed a heart desiring to do the right thing by pleasing God and others. At this point in my religious conviction, I felt pretty good about myself and was convinced that being a good person was all I needed to earn my spot in heaven. The seed however was planted, and I knew seeking a heartfelt type of religious experience with God driven by love and appreciation was what I needed rather than the fear, guilt and difficulties motivating my earlier years. This period of my life helped me understand that learning is a lifelong process that provides each of us with experiences to help us to grow physically, emotionally and spiritually. As we are exposed to new situations, it is critical to begin each endeavor with a strong foundation and good support system. The values I gained early in life such as honesty, integrity, faith, love for others, and a sense of responsibility for my actions have formed my personality and molded my character. The values from my early formative years continued to develop as I have added the desire to cultivate my personal relationship with God and others. Beginning during childhood and continuing through adolescence and adulthood we are presented with experiences where we learn the importance of creating lasting relationships with families, friends and our teachers. Along with growing and learning comes the responsibility to apply what we learn to how we live our lives. Exposure to new experiences such as friendships, careers, spiritual experiences, and recreational activities opens the door to new ways of thinking and acting.

Over time and as a result of the experiences in my life, I realize how actions from the heart are more impactful and more lasting than those from habit.

Run To Faith

Chapter Five

Leaving the Nest

"Like a bird that strays from its nest is a man who strays from his home." Proverbs 27:8

Don't be last... don't be last... don't be last. That's all that I could think while I dug deep and tried to maintain my pace heading into the woods for the last half mile of the race. A four mile time trial just before Labor Day is a tradition which signifies the start of a new cross-country season at Eastern Michigan University. After the run, the team is treated to a barbecue lunch and brief meeting in which plans for the season are reviewed and the new runners are welcomed. Eastern Michigan University is respected as a national power in men's track and cross-country producing numerous All-

Americans, Olympians, and nationally ranked teams. A differentiator of the Eastern team philosophy compared to its rivals is that anyone who wants to run is welcomed to be a part of the team and can proudly wear the legendary green and white of EMU. This contrasts the approach of the majority of big name teams who have strict limits on the number of runners on their roster. This philosophy has worked well for EMU Coach Bob Parks who recognizes how runners tend to mature at different times. Experience showed him that kids could enter his program from inadequate high school programs or they may be slow starters who mature late with dramatic progress. As a walk-on, I was awed by the talent and tradition that surrounded me.   In addition to the returning runners who had qualified for the NCAA Division 1 Nationals the previous year, there was a strong contingent of national class high school runners that included Nick Ellis, a 8:55 two-miler and Golden West Champion, Dave Burkhart a 4:11 miler, Rick Goodman, a 4:16 miler, and Bob Hunt who finished second in the Michigan high school state meet two mile with a 9:03. My new teammates were the guys I read about in the local newspaper.

I crossed the finish line of my four-mile time trial with a time of 23:08. I was satisfied that I beat a couple runners and also had raced a four-mile for the first time—setting a personal best. This was the point where I set my first personal goal to be competitive. I had no visions of cracking the top seven but felt if I could only improve to sub twenty-two, I would move up to the middle of the pack. Over the next year, I made the transformation into a collegiate runner by gradually increasing my mileage from 40 to 70 miles a week. The progression didn't come easily. I typically returned home well after the majority of my teammates. Much to my dismay, the increased mileage resulted in little improvement during that first year. I recalled a team ten-mile run early in the year where I ran out of energy and walked the last three miles, missing dinner and collapsing on my bed. I met with similar experiences much of that year but continued to plug away, refusing to quit.   I was proud to wear my EMU track hoodie and had high hopes that track would be different. The format of college track meets includes a large number of middle-distance events. These events allow for many runners, especially half-milers to compete. I focused my training on speed work, in hopes of earning a spot on the relays. I progressed to the point where my time of 1:55 was good enough to fill out a couple relays and was rewarded when our squad finished first in the 1973 Central Collegiate indoor track championships. Much like cross-country, EMU has always been nationally ranked as a powerhouse in track and field. Legends from the past included Olympic gold medalist Hayes Jones and Olympian Dave Ellis. During my tenure, the roster included Olympic 100-meter Gold Medalist Hasley Crawford, world-class quarter-milers Stan Vinson and Eugene Thomas, and world-ranked, twenty-eight-minute 10,000-meter, distance star Gordon Minty. Future stars included 1500-Meter Olympian Paul McMullen, 800-meter Olympic silver medalist Earl Jones, distance star Boaz Cheryobo, high-jumper Jamie Nietro, and many more.

The camaraderie between distance runners was unique. Whether you were 1st or 30th, you were welcomed as an essential part of the team. The early morning runs, team breakfasts, post-race get-togethers, card games and five-hour bus rides were a special part of my college years and resulted in life-long friendships. As we grew closer, our mornings began with non-scheduled distance runs, our days filled with classes, afternoon practice, team workouts followed by dinner, work and studying. Before the end of each day, we would make plans to meet at the corner of Huron and LeForge at eight o'clock for five-to-ten mile runs. The new slogan that can be seen throughout Michigan seemed to summarize how we felt: "True EMU".

The number of relationships and friendships among my teammates grew to include several distance running stars such as Tom Hollander, Brian Williams, Terry Furst, Scott Hubbard, Dave Burkhart, and Maurice Weaver, as well as world-class hurdler and

400-meter runner Jeff Dils, and decathlete Gary Bastien.   They were not only my teammates then, they are still my friends today.

As the indoor season wound down, it was apparent there really was no off-season for a college-level distance runner. Cross-country transitioned into indoor track which transitioned into outdoor track. If you wanted to be ready for cross-country, you needed to build a mileage base over the summer to handle the upcoming fall cross-country workouts. I learned that two-a-day workouts were an important part of training, regardless of the season. That summer I was convinced the high mileage my faster teammates had been doing for years was the key to their success, so I worked up to ninety to one hundred miles per week. When cross-country started, I felt sluggish but excited about seeing what kind of results my hard work would produce. I became very consistent at running in the mid 21's for four miles and thirty-two to thirty-three minutes for the 10K—not good enough for Varsity, but much better than a year ago. I still lagged behind the lead group in races and workouts. I worked hard but seemed to have plateaued and wondered if this was as good as I could be. My track season was similar in that I showed steady progress and made contributions to the team. However nothing was spectacular. My times improved to 1:53 for the half mile, 3:01 for the three-quarter mile and 4:16 for the mile.   The highlight of that season was qualifying for and participating in the NCAA two-mile relay, although our team failed to qualify for the finals.

I patiently continued to work hard throughout the competitive year and summer. After enduring a summer of high mileage and quality workouts I had high hopes for my junior year in cross-country. Several upperclassmen graduated from the team which had placed 6th in the NCAA Nationals from the prior year. When I toed the line for the first five-mile race, I felt ready and excited to make a leap into the top seven and earn a spot on the coveted travel squad.   Once the gun sounded, I was dismayed to feel heavy and sluggish legs. My time in that first race of 26:20 was respectable but discouraging since I had hoped for much more.   I maintained a similar performance level most of the year putting me anywhere from 7th to 9th man on the team. As the year wound down, I was on the edge, but not quite able to crack into the top seven to earn the privilege of competing in the Conference, Regional, and National meets.

I was tired and discouraged!! Two straight years of running 100 miles a week had resulted in some track success but little gain in cross-country. When the squad was announced for the District Regionals and I was left off, I decided to quit. I stopped going to practice and didn't run a step for the next three weeks, not sure if I would ever return to the team.

Despite my decision to take a leave from my running, the friendships with my teammates remained. I encouraged my teammates as they performed well during the conference and championship races finishing first in the MidAmerican Conference and 21st during the National Championships. After a couple weeks respite, I regained my desire to run. Over the next several days, I did a little jogging and decided to run a low-key, open-meet, four-mile race that was sponsored by EMU on our home course. The Eastern Michigan University cross-country course of the mid-1970's was the epitome of home-field advantage. The course was located behind the historic Bowen Field House/Warner Gymnasium complex which housed our indoor track, basketball court, swimming pool, wrestling and gymnastic venues. Located in the middle of the first loop were the varsity tennis courts. The far end of the course meandered around the soccer and intramural fields and several dormitories. The end loop circled the married housing complex. The course was distinguished by many quick turns, a small wooded area, and several slight up and down hills. A strategic section of the course ran along the side of a hill where passing was close to impossible. A real plus to the course is that spectators could easily watch an entire race.

Coach Parks has kept all-time lists of every event in track and field on every course and every distance. He has a formula to convert yards to meters, miles to kilometers and a rating factor of cross-country course difficulty from which he adjusts runner's times. Anyone who has ever run for EMU can easily obtain their placing on the all-time list with all of these differences factored in. As I toed the line, my position on the list based upon my best time of 21:26 was somewhere between one hundred-fifty and one hundred-sixty.

Like many road races, you never know who is going to show up.   Past participants include such running greats as Boston Marathon champion Greg Meyer, marathon legend Doug Kurtis, Tennessee All-American Pat Davey, former Michigan standout Mike McGuire, and a number of legendary Eastern Michigan runners. The race included a variety of runners including participants from junior colleges, high-schools, and recently graduated alumni.

As the starting gun sounded, I felt relaxed and refreshed and began with a quick-starting reaction. I quickly moved into the second pack where I settled in for the first mile. Passing the mile in just under five minutes, I felt exceptionally strong and surprised at the ease of the pace. Nearing the tennis courts, we approached two miles in about ten minutes flat. This was a good thirty seconds better than I had ever done before, but surprisingly I felt even better. At that point, I put down my head and quickly closed the gap on the   leaders as we headed for the soccer fields and the three mile mark.   Easing into the lead and for the first time in my running memories, I decided to push the pace and see who would follow. By the time we headed toward the married housing complex, with a half mile to go, I had become unaware of anyone else's location and began my sprint to the finish. I crossed the finish line and for the first time in my life was handed a wooden Popsicle stick with the number one- a first place finish. When I walked along the path past the finish area, I was informed that I had run 20:06, good enough for fourth on the all-time four-mile course list. A feeling of confident euphoria came over me while I was congratulated by Coach Parks. I could see in his eyes the excitement of knowing that a runner in his program had come from being an unrecruited walk-on to a potential front-runner.

I had one more opportunity to test myself and validate my performance, as our official season had ended and we were quickly approaching the indoor track season. I discovered that the United States Track and Field Federation National Cross-County Championships, a now defunct organization—that was popular in the 1970's was scheduled at the University of Michigan in Ann Arbor the next week. Along with a number of teammates that were hoping for a good season-ending performance, we entered and made the grueling seven-mile trip to Ann Arbor for the Thanksgiving weekend race. As the race began, I felt the cold rain that accompanied the thirty-five degree morning. The course was extremely muddy and slippery, which I looked at as an advantage. I felt the extreme conditions would slow fast runners to the point that I could be competitive. Running near the front of the pack for most of the race I was ecstatic to finish 11th and earn All-American honors that went with being a top-fifteen finisher. According to Coach, my time of 31:02 for 10K was impressive and through his formula would translate to a 30:20. The actual time put me in the top twenty-five on the all-time EMU list. With my new found energy and confidence, I was ready for indoor track!

****

I stood at the counter of the automobile repair shop awaiting the prognosis of repairs needed for my 1965 Mustang.

"Three hundred dollars? A new water pump? Well, I can't pay you until next Friday—but if it needs to get done, I guess you may as well fix it." I had returned from a trip to Ann Arbor and noticed the temperature gauge skyrocket to the red zone. A few minutes later I was standing by the side of Washtenaw Avenue watching steam pour from the engine compartment. I bought the Mustang from a co-worker in high school for $400.00. What a deal. However, over two years, about half of my paychecks went to keeping it running. I had a tight budget, trying to earn enough money through a variety of odd jobs to pay tuition, rent, food, and other necessities of college life; such as decent running shoes and a subscription to "Track and Field News".

My parents were supportive and proud of my drive to earn a college degree. However they never quite understood my desire to run and thought of it as a waste of time. Their parents had grown up during the great depression of the 1920's and lived a difficult life. They were used to long hours of work—something that was passed down to my parents. My father viewed running as something reserved for children. "When are you going to grow up and stop running?" he would ask me whenever I came home.

His attitude, like many of his generation, was that work defined who you were. He worked ten hours a day, six days a week, and my mother cared for the house and six children, leaving little time or money to support my pursuit of a college degree. Their home was always open to me. However, the day they dropped me off at school, my first day of college, was the day I was on my own.

The budgeting of my finances left me little room for anything extra, so the car had to wait. During my first couple of years at school, I quickly learned if I didn't absolutely need something, I would have to pass on it, an attribute that has carried itself throughout my life. I quickly established a reputation for being frugal with my money, something I became proud of.

I was a good student in high school and as I approached graduation, I was determined to attend college. Attending college was rare in the 1970's in Detroit and the number of students from Cody High School, who went on to higher education was about 10%. I had no idea what kind of career I would pursue but knew that my options for a fulfilling work life would be greatly improved with a college degree. Skipping college, most of my of my high-school friends and classmates were anxious to get high-paying jobs in the auto factories that surrounded the Detroit area. Factory jobs were easy to come by, paid well, and enabled a decent lifestyle that included new cars, apartments, and enough money to enjoy the nightlife.

To afford my first year of college, I depleted the savings I earned from my part-time, high-school jobs, took student loans, received a few academic scholarships and worked multiple part-time jobs. My teammates were amazed I was able to work multiple jobs, run twice a day, and study fifteen credit hours while maintaining a 3.5 grade point average. I often wondered how others could not excel in academics if they had no jobs and did not spend three to four hours a day practicing a skill or sport. Looking back, I feel the greatest personal characteristic I obtained from college life was not the technical knowledge used in my subsequent career, but the discipline to prioritize my life for success.

While I walked home from the repair shop, I reflected upon my situation. I had second thoughts about whether this lifestyle was worth the effort. I felt a bit of jealousy toward my high-school friends who had little financial worries, plenty of money, and plenty of time to enjoy themselves. I was jealous of other students who were financially supported by their parents. I contemplated quitting on my educational goals and joining the workforce.

Struggling to be at peace, I prayed to God that night to guide me through this difficult time.

I awoke to a sunny, warm day and prepared to meet a couple of my teammates at the corner for our seven-mile morning run. Not a cloud was in the sky as I opened the door of the apartment and began jogging to our meeting spot. As we started the run, I thought briefly about my troubles, but the conversation quickly helped me forget. The run was great and we talked about jumping in the apartment swimming pool for a quick swim before heading to class. A feeling of peacefulness came over me as I pushed the pace entering the last mile. Friendship, the enjoyment of running, the swimming pool, all helped me realize what made me happy were life's simple things, not cars, TVs or parties. The Lord had answered my prayer and opened my eyes.

Returning to my classes, my job, track practice, friends, and studies I was thankful to the Lord for blessing me with my talents and current situation. I gained an appreciation for all of these things, knowing that worldly possessions do not bring joy and contentment. I realized my outlook is the key characteristic that enables happiness and contentment. Appreciation grew for my busy schedule which helped to shield me from distractions that could lead me down the wrong path. Like any college, EMU was loaded with opportunities to party, use drugs, and imbibe in excessive drinking. Knowing I had a ten-mile run scheduled for the next day, a big meet, an exam, or a job helped me limit those extra-curricular activities. If I was going to make this work, I needed discipline. As the year continued, I realized I was going to have trouble staying on track on my own. I remembered I had support from Jesus Christ whenever I needed it and I was going to take advantage of that gift.

My spiritual upbringing taught me belonging to a congregation of believers is an important motivating factor for being a good Christian, so I sought out a church. A couple of teammates encouraged me to join them at the campus church "Holy Trinity" chapel and I complied. Holy Trinity was unlike the traditional services I knew as a child and teenager. The mass followed the agenda of a typical traditional service. However the messages seemed more relevant to real life than I expected, focusing on relating to the challenges of young adult college students. Being a Christian was much more than putting in my time on Sunday morning, rather something I was at all times. The services were inspiring and left me with a desire to learn more and return the following week. I felt spiritually fulfilled but failed to grasp the importance of Jesus dying for our sins as being the key to my faith. I felt if I was good enough that I would gain salvation.

Moving away from the familiar surroundings of home to college can provide the opportunity to broaden your perspective of the world. As your world becomes larger, so do the challenges. In athletics, the performance level of athletes raises the bar dramatically compared to high school competition. Academically there is the realization of how competitive the school and work environment is. To succeed, challenges need to be faced head on while continuing to strive toward your goals. The results may not be what you expect. However staying the course allows you to be the best you can be. When things get difficult, the key to overcoming hurdles is determining priorities and having the discipline to make the right choices. As you move through life, new situations and environments provide challenges for growing spiritually in the absence of the reinforcement and support of home life. The good news is you don't have to go it alone. Friends and family may come and go, but Jesus Christ is always there to help and support you.

Run To Faith

Chapter Six

Having a Plan – Training to Achieve Your Goals

"May He grant all your heart's desire and fulfill all your plans!" Psalms 20:4

As I neared the end of lap six, I was positioned right where I wanted to be—just behind the leaders and in striking distance for the win. My sprinting speed was average so starting my finishing kick sooner than my competitors gave me the best chance to win. I typically moved into my desired position with about 440 yards to go. I tried to build a lead, set the pace, and to keep it going to hold off my competition during the final strides of the race. I passed the lead runners and my thoughts returned to last Wednesday's workout.

My planned workout was to run eight, quarter-mile repeats at race pace. I had finished number eight right on pace—60.5 seconds. My legs ached with fatigue, but I felt pleasantly tired while I walked a few seconds and began my cool-down with some easy jogging around the indoor track. While jogging along the backstretch I glanced up at the EMU track record board and imagined seeing my name there among all of the legendary runners who have called Bowen Fieldhouse their home. Bowen Fieldhouse is an icon of indoor track, similar to Lambeau Field of the Green Bay Packers, Wrigley Field of the Cubs, and Fenway Park of the Red Sox. It is a dark venue with a weathered green track that is as hard as a paved road. Bleachers surround the track and are pulled out for home basketball games. The hallway to the locker room sports a bulletin board where the daily track workout, schedule, and track meet lineups are posted.

Indoor track meets are an intimate experience at EMU as a balcony overhangs the track and puts spectators in the middle of the action. When I made my way around the 220-yard track, my mind told me that I could do just a little more. Instead of going to my sweats for a cool-down, I hit the starting line, reset my watch and began an additional repeat 440. I fought through the fatigue and settled into a fast but controlled pace. Fatigue began to set in as I reached the backstretch, but I continued to fight and lengthened my stride... 29.5—good pace but is it too much? I put down my head, pumped my arms and worked through the next lap finishing in 58.5. I bent over to catch my breath, feeling queasy but satisfied. "You okay, Jim?" shouted coach Parks.

"Just enjoying the moment" I replied. I kept reminding myself while I gasped and began to walk. I thought, "The harder I work now, the more it will pay off later." Once again, I began a slow jog around the track. When I neared the completion of my lap, I thought to myself "What the heck, you can do another." I hit the line and started again. "Pain is good, pain means success!" I told myself as I summoned all of my strength to complete the interval. The fatigue made me oblivious to my pace. I just ran hard. "28.5" ... "wow—keep it going!" I thought. My legs tightened around the last turn and I pumped hard to the finish. "58.2!" No more jogging... I couldn't take another. I composed myself and walked a lap before going to the drinking fountain and then out the door for my two-mile jog home.

"Great workout," I thought to myself, trying to build my confidence for next week's conference championships. I was cautious about being overjoyed remembering there are no awards for good workouts and my ultimate goal was to win the Mid-American Conference one-mile run the following week.

Quarter-mile repeats were always something I could handle. As much as I struggled over the years with repeat miles, hills, tempo runs, and long distance training, I had always been able to hold my own doing quarter-mile repeats. Mixed in with the right combination of distance training and faster speed work, I attribute much of my running improvement to quarter-mile repeats. They gave me confidence and allowed me to push myself harder than many other workouts. Quarters not only built speed, but helped me to relax and run more efficiently at the longer distances. Therefore, I embraced them as my strength and key workout. When comparing my training to my teammates, I quickly noticed that runners often end up with similar results, even though their workout plan is very different. My world-class teammate Gordon Minty thrived on long distance training covering twenty miles a day. His training consistency resulted in great success in cross-country and longer distances as well as a 4:03 personal best in the mile.

My teammate Tom Hollander thrived on long intervals that resulted in an 8:40 two mile and 4:07 mile. Mark Smith was a world class steeplechaser on thirty to thirty-five miles per week. Like many areas of life, each person is a unique individual and learns to leverage their strengths for best results. In retrospect, my improvement at finishing ten-mile runs and becoming more competitive during cross-country mile-repeat workouts was probably a sign I was ready for a breakthrough on the track. Mentally, the hardest part of doing all of this work was the patience it took to endure the endless miles of foundation work that strengthened my body and contributed to my overall fitness level.

During my downtime from running, work, and school I enjoyed reading the latest Track and Field News and Runners World magazines. The new training secrets that were published in each issue were amusing. My first impression was they were targeted at novice runners looking for a shortcut or trick to quickly improve their running performance. As an experienced runner, I was able to recognize the merit of the schedules and techniques published, but also understood a strong foundation included the right balance of long distance strength work, the tuning provided by speed work and the recovery through adequate rest. Over the years, I realized the twenty-week marathon program or "ten weeks to your first 5K schedules" were proven techniques that provided the right balance and type of workouts depending upon the runner's goals. Results were certain to improve by following these programs. However, results would vary based upon a runner's fitness level when starting the program and the dedication and effort put into each workout. Regardless of the goal and the training schedule, each program included the proper balance of distance, speed, and rest to achieve that specific goal. What I was able to take away from these schedules and advice is that there are no shortcuts to success. Adding specificity to training equals a greater chance of obtaining the desired results. Subsequently, I have found the advice from expert coaches and articles have helped me to adapt my training as my goals varied to run 5Ks, 10K, half, and full marathons. Adapting training to deal with the demands of family, work, relationships, aging, energy level, and injury has also been a key factor in successfully balancing running into life. There is no substitute for hard work. Keeping it fun and enjoying the journey means easy runs, cross training, and adequate rest days.

My workouts building up to the race that night had helped to position me right where I wanted to be. When I passed the finish line with two laps remaining in the Mid-American Conference one-mile race, I counted on my training to carry me through the last quarter-mile ahead of the field. I swung to the outside and accelerated to move past the group and into the lead. My momentum helped me build a five-yard lead down the backstretch. I rounded the turn and headed into the final lap, reacting to another surge of energy as the gun sounded to signify the final lap. Recalling the effort needed to finish last Wednesday's workout I knew what I could do. Digging deep, I fought the fatigue in my legs which carried me over the finish line as the winner of the Mid-American Conference championship race. Knowing that I did the work, ran the race, and earned the right to claim this race for me and my teammates was satisfying.

Later in life, the need to adapt my training to a new distance became evident since I had set my goal of running a sub 2:30 marathon at the Detroit Free Press Marathon. After twenty-six miles, I eyed the finish line when I entered the final straightaway knowing I had little left. The roar of the crowd encouraged me to dig deep and use my remaining energy to propel myself to the finish line. Until mile twenty-four, I had allocated my energy properly and was well below the planned pace to reach my goal. I then got first-hand experience of hitting the "wall". Digging deep I felt somewhat energetic climbing the only real hill on the course- a half-mile climb onto Belle Isle Park. Coming off the hill I worked hard and I passed two runners moving into 5th place. Before the finish, the course took runners for an additional loop into the park for the final two miles. In the distance, I could see the banners and hear the crowd that lined the finish area. Silence soon returned as I made my way away from the crowd attempting to complete the race. The drop in adrenalin and accompanying fatigue soon overtook my body as I struggled to keep my legs moving.

Throughout my running career, I raced many distances and found that both my talent and desire left me better suited for half-mile and the one mile on the track rather than the longer distances. As the years after college graduation passed, the opportunities to compete on the track dwindled and I transitioned to road racing. Varied success came from my attempt to adapt to the longer distances. Workouts were adjusted to run competitively with longer runs, hills, and long intervals.   My core workout of quarter-mile repeats helped with running efficiency however didn't provide me with the endurance foundation needed to finish strong at the longer distances. Key workouts for five and ten kilometer distances became hills and hard ten-mile runs. As most of my running partners began running on the roads rather than the track, all would share their stories about the joy of running the marathon. After enough prodding, I finally gave in by entering my first marathon. My friends helped to lay out a three-month program building upon my base of sixty miles a week. Three weeks into the program made me feel like this was an entirely different sport than the one I had grown to know and love over the past several years. I struggled with the patience it took to run for three hours or recover from the fatigue of a twenty-miler. In the spring of 1979, I entered my first marathon in Cleveland, Ohio. My memory of the days following the race has become one that sticks in my mind and resurfaces any time I have the slightest notion to do it again. Despite what I thought was an acceptable time of 2:38 the week-long soreness that followed the effort left me with little desire to do it again.

However, living the adage that time heals all wounds I found myself convinced to see what I could do five years later. I hoped to learn from my initial experience where my speed had helped me to relax and feel comfortable for twenty-two miles before crashing and just hoping to finish. My plan was to dedicate six months toward gaining the endurance I felt I needed to finish strong. My goal race was decided for the fall, reasoning that summer would be much easier to endure long runs than the brutal Michigan winters. I heeded the advice of published training programs that recommended building up slowly to multiple twenty-plus mile training runs while incorporating a mix of long intervals to support a fast but relaxed pace.

After researching finish times of the past several Detroit marathons, I set a goal pace by reasoning that a 2:30 or slightly faster than a six-minute-mile pace would get me into the top twenty finishers. As the gun sounded, signifying the start of the Detroit Free Press Marathon, I remembered to hold back, relax and run the first ten miles as a fast training run, shooting for a time of fifty-seven minutes. Reducing my mileage over the past couple of weeks had left me feeling surprisingly fresh and I was elated to hear fifty-six minutes when I passed the ten mile mark. "Run another ten-miler just like that." I encouraged myself as I continued on the course. My pace was a consistent 5:40 per mile which left me feeling confident and strong while I continued to pass participants and move up toward the leaders.

The race was going according to plan as I passed mile twenty at 1:52, exactly 5:40 per mile pace. "Now the race begins," I thought. "If I can just run six-minute per mile pace I'll beat my goal." I continued with my consistent pace when I neared the bridge and mile twenty-four. "You're in seventh—keep it up" I heard from the spectators. I was also advised that I had moved to within two minutes of the leaders. I recalled my track strategy of beginning my kick early in order to move into position and hold off the competition. This is when the realization of how a one-mile race and marathon differ.   I accelerated on the hill and I became overwhelmed with a quick drain of energy. Unlike the mile where guts and focus could get me to the finish, I had little left to finish strong. Working as hard as I could, I struggled for what seemed like an eternity over the last fifteen minutes to finish in 2:29:02.   I was elated to achieve my goal as well as learn the lesson about tailoring my preparation for maximizing my performance.

Without a proven plan, I would have had little chance of accomplishing my goal that day.   I enjoyed the experience. However, unlike the majority of my running partners who have run well over one hundred marathons each, I continue to enjoy adventures in running by focusing on a variety of events, all much shorter than twenty-six miles.

The following eight steps help guide you to get the most from your preparation.

1.   Be patient, life is a marathon, not a sprint. Setting difficult but attainable goals along the way will help ensure you keep your spirit alive.

2.   Don't expect to dive right in and be successful. You need to build a strong foundation to handle the more difficult workouts and tasks that will follow.

3.   Figure out what kind of specific training, practices, and workouts will help you attain your goal. Training for a marathon and an 800-meter race is very different, so the proper mix is important.

4.   Figure out your strengths and leverage them to meet your goal.

5.   Your mission is to achieve your goal. There are no awards for doing great workouts in themselves, only in using them in your goal race or life situations.

6.   Listen to your body and mind. You can't go hard all the time. Be sure to incorporate rest and relaxation along the way.

7.   Refuel and refresh. Be sure to feed yourself with physical and spiritual nutrition to remain energetic and strong.

8.   Find partners who have similar goals who will work with and encourage you.

****

On a beautiful October evening in 2013, with unseasonably warm temperatures and plenty of late day sunshine, I gathered wood for the fire. My wife and I volunteered to entertain our small church group during our monthly activity night by hosting a bonfire and a few outdoor games. Deb and I belonged to a number of small church groups since joining Grace Church, a non-denominational Bible-based Christian church twelve years prior. We found that changing groups occasionally provided us the benefits of experiencing differing perspectives about life and spirituality as well as gave us the opportunity to grow our relationships. Two years ago we had been asked to help begin a ministry for the mobile-home community across the field adjacent to our church. The goal of the ministry was to reach out to our neighbors, establish relationships, and spread the message of the Bible. We've had varied success, however, have achieved the intended result of forming relationships and friendships with the dozen or so members who regularly attend our weekly Bible study.

Belonging to the group has impacted my relationship with Jesus Christ by opening my eyes to both the needy and privileged in our community. As the group gathered that October evening, I volunteered to begin the evening in prayer. Over the last several years, my skills and confidence have grown in a number of areas including my understanding of the teachings of Christ, living my life as a Christian, and learning to pray in a meaningful way.

During my early experiences in a small group setting, my comfort level was somewhat low. The gatherings were culturally different than any experience I could remember. Despite my uneasiness, I was encouraged by my wife to attend a small group and see if things got better. The people were warm and friendly; however, I remained uneasy with this new routine. There were parts of the usual meeting agenda that came easier to me than others. The typical agenda for the small group meetings consisted of a period of socializing, time to review and discuss Bible passages and themes, and prayer. Review and discussions about Bible passages were insightful and enjoyable. I quickly found that the more I studied, the more I strived to learn about the life and teachings of Jesus.

Over time, I grew increasingly comfortable as the group shared food, stories, and experiences with one another, but when it came time to offer up prayer or prayer requests, I was still uneasy. Prayer requests from the group ranged from traumatic events such as severe illnesses, death, job loss, divorce, etc... to minor issues like moving to a new house, having a cold, or car repair issues. I sensed that members often just wanted to share their feelings about life's events, troubles, and concerns. Regardless of the topic or level of seriousness, all prayer requests were respected and addressed.

At that time in my life, I felt that God had better things to worry about than my insignificant problems. The world is consumed with events such as shootings, catastrophic weather, wars, droughts, criminal activity, and families losing their life savings... "My problems are insignificant compared to what is going on in the world around me," I thought. I had not yet understood that God cares and hears all and that all requests are important to Him.

When the prayer portion of the meeting began, I hung my head and listened to members of the group who volunteered to pray. The prayers were deep and sincere and for the first fifteen minutes or so, I was attentive and engaged, but the repetition often broke down my concentration and I became anxious. "I am empathetic, but please get to the point," I thought to myself. The memory of these prayer sessions left an impression on me... that as I approached prayer, I would strive to be sincere, honest, and engage in short, to-the-point sessions rather than being repetitive and searching for eloquent words. I thought about the common repetitive verses that I memorized as a child, the heartfelt but repetitive messages in these meetings, and determined that I would get the most out of developing my own style that was characterized by informal sincerity, much like conversing with a friend or acquaintance. Despite this revelation, I was still missing the point as I felt that prayer was something that God wanted us to do to make us suffer and learn discipline.

Over the course of the next few years, I studied God's Word in earnest by reading a number of Christian books, reading the Bible, and attending numerous small church groups. The key message that transformed my outlook on prayer came from these teachings. I learned that the Bible not only instructs us to pray, but to pray with joy from the heart as evidenced by several Bible passages. *"I thank my God in all my remembrances of you; always in every prayer of mine for you all making my prayer with joy, because of your partnership in the gospel from the first day until* now."- Philippians 1:4-5. "For you may very well be giving thanks well enough but the other person is not being built up"- 1 Corinthians 14:17. The Bible teaches us to pray to be thankful, to praise the Lord, and to ask God for strength to do His will. It teaches us to praise the Lord not only quietly in our hearts, but also aloud so that others too can join in thanks. It also teaches us not to pray selfishly. "Yet even when you do pray, your prayers are not answered because you pray just for selfish reasons"- James 4:3.

Then it finally hit me! We are guided to pray as Jesus instructed in the Gospel by keeping it simple, real, and having it come from the heart. "And when you pray, you must not be like the hypocrites. For they love to stand and pray in the synagogues and at the street corners, that they may be seen by others. Truly, I say to you, they have received their reward. But when you pray, go into your room and shut the door and pray to your Father who is in secret. And your Father who sees in secret will reward you. And when you pray, do not heap up empty phrases as the Gentiles do, for they think that they will be heard for their many words. Do not be like them, for your Father knows what you need before you ask him." Matthew 6:5-8

When I thought about prayer, the popular adage "Practice Makes Perfect" came to mind. This theme worked well for me in other areas of life, so why not here? I took my new approach to prayer and practiced.

At our daily meals, our family replaced our usual memorized prayer with a prayer that came from the heart... anything that came to mind as we reflected upon the day. I discovered that praying each night when I prepared to sleep was a good time to reflect upon the events of the day and have a conversation with God.

When I lay down to sleep, I begin a quiet conversation with God thanking Him for all He has given to me and my family. I share with Him my thoughts and problems.

At holidays and extended family gatherings, prayer time has become a collection of thank-yous and requests from the family to God. Adding regular prayer to my daily ritual has helped me to view God as I would my Father or best friend... someone who is always there for me. I often prayed to Him that He will help me to understand His plan, the significance of the Death and Resurrection of Jesus, and strengthen me to please Him.

Over time, focused practice turns into habits that extend all areas of life. The struggle of finding time for prayer or wondering if prayer is good enough gradually disappears. Instead of being a once-a-day or once-a-week event, prayer has become a continual part of my life. I mentally converse with Jesus when I awake, when I eat, while driving to work, while running, while hiking. Anywhere, anytime.

I discovered that my goal is not the praying itself but how it strengthens my desire to apply thoughts and revelations practically through actions. Reflecting upon a situation and asking God for guidance has helped me react in a Christian manner when encountering life's challenges. Similar to training for running by running more to reach my athletic goals, praying has helped me to move closer to God and reach my spiritual goals. Much like with running, practicing this lifestyle becomes easier over time.

I volunteered to pray in our Bible groups and over time it feels easier, more enjoyable, and more meaningful. I no longer worry about saying the right words... I just say what is on my mind. An unanticipated benefit is that a number of others who were reluctant to pray have followed my lead by offering short, but meaningful prayers during our time together.

As the group arrived that October night, I started the bonfire. Our group leader addressed everyone by suggesting we start with an opening prayer. I quickly interjected that I would like to lead the prayer. My plan was to pray in a way that would involve everyone by having them feel comfortable enough to join in. "Can we all just start by telling God what we are thankful for?... Anything at all..." There was silence for a few moments when I quickly added, "God, Thank you for leading us to this group, for you have provided me with the gift of friendship and the opportunity to meet some wonderful people... and thank you God for the food we will share because I love the way it tastes." Everyone smiled and quickly joined in with their special prayers of thanks.

One member prayed that her children would embrace God as their savior and become involved in a church congregation. One prayed for the health of her daughter. Another prayed for strength to address struggles with co-workers. Someone else prayed for a safe trip for their family. We all prayed with the comfort of knowing that God heard our prayers and will address them not on our terms but in a way that is best for us.

Achieving goals often takes hard work, discipline, and patience. Keeping it simple and adding the right amount of fun and enjoyment can enhance the experience. Yet, without a good plan the chances of reaching your goals are slim. Over time, practicing the right things will eventually lead you closer to your goal. Researching training programs or engaging a coach or teammates with similar goals can help provide the roadmap you need to achieve your goals. Similarly, seeking out the Word of God through the Bible, Religious Books, and Bible studies is essential to understanding how to draw nearer to God.

Patience is important and you shouldn't expect instant results. Your body and mind require dedication to your plan that starts with a strong foundation, practice, and application of these principles. Keep in mind your ultimate goal is not to be a workout champion, but to apply your training principles on race day and in real life

Run To Faith

Chapter Seven

Continuing the Journey –
Ensuring the Proper Balance

"Ponder the path of your feet; then all your ways will be sure." Proverbs 4:26

In 1980, there were limited opportunities in Southeast Michigan for post-collegiate athletes to continue to compete in track and field. The majority of distance runners who pursued high-level competition at the national and international level relocated to the few areas that initially set the standard for accommodating elite training groups; including Boulder Colorado, Boston Massachusetts, Gainesville Florida, Colorado Springs Colorado, San

Diego California, and Eugene Oregon.

As the running boom of the 1980's progressed, a number of area clubs began to form and grow their membership numbers. However, the majority focused on the fun-run and age-group population who participated in 10K road races. Many serious distance runners who remained in the area after graduation discovered a home with the Ann Arbor Track Club whose membership included a wide range of talent and ages. The Ann Arbor Track Club provided coaching and structured workouts gauged to the varying talent level of its members. The openness to all levels of runners was key to the club's growth and in 2015, it remains strong in numbers. As a result of the success of area distance runners such as Olympians Earl Jones, Paul McMullen, Brian Diemer, and Kevin Sullivan, the Ann Arbor area has become a renown distance running location. Meanwhile, thirty miles away in Rochester Michigan, brothers Kevin and Keith Hanson, who started a local running apparel store while coaching high school track, began the Hanson Running Project. This project provided financial support to elite distance runners which allowed them to focus on training and competition. The growth of success in both Ann Arbor and Rochester transformed Southeast Michigan into a prominent destination for elite distance runners to call home.

Back in the early 1980's the Ann Arbor Track Club offered competitive runners the opportunity to continue training with partners who hoped to stay in the area and continue to compete on the track. Landing my first full-time job on the campus of Eastern Michigan University in neighboring Ypsilanti, the club helped me pursue my passion in my hometown. The setting provided me with access to workout facilities, coaching, and fellow runners that were critical to my pursuit. Over time, I adapted to a new workout schedule that included lunch-time runs and evening workouts on the track.

I continued my training with the same intensity as I had in college. My weekly mileage hovered between seventy-five to eighty miles and consisted of two-a-day workouts in the form of daily distance runs and various types of speed work. I remained competitive but lost the edge I had during college, as my mile times slowed from 4:04 to a consistent 4:10 and 880 from 1:49 to 1:53. After a period of consistent but slower races, I searched for an answer wondering if at the age of twenty-five my best days were behind me.

In the past, working harder was the key ingredient to my steady improvement. However, that wasn't working now. Knowing that I needed to tweak my approach to training to reach my goals, I tried something new. Instead of working as hard as I could, I finally woke up and listened to my body... and my heart. The cornerstone of my new approach entailed quality over quantity, ensuring that I gave myself adequate recovery to achieve my planned workout times. By lowering my mileage by twenty percent to sixty miles per week and increasing recovery days, I felt new energy that resulted in better workouts and eventually a dramatic improvement in race-day performance.

I stepped to the starting line on a January Friday night in 1980 at Bowen Fieldhouse and awaited the starters signal. When the gun sounded to signify the start of the one mile run, I felt the freshness and confidence that I had lacked during the past two seasons. My racing strategy was different than in college where my primary goal was to win races for my team by competing in several races per night. That strategy was to position myself behind the leaders; keep within striking range, and move to the lead with a long kick, saving as much energy as possible to win the event and be ready for my next race. My new strategy was simply to get to the lead and see how fast I could run. My goal was to break the record of 4:03 which had been set by the 1972 Olympic, 800-meter-champion Dave Wottle several years ago.

I quickly moved into the lead, passing the first quarter mile in fifty-seven seconds. "Wow – this would be a good start for an 880." I thought to myself. I maintained my pace remembering to relax and run hard. When I approached the half-way point, I heard the next split time. "1:58!" The crowd was roaring hoping to see the first sub-four minute mile in Bowen Field House history. I reminded myself to relax and just keep it going.

My next lap (thirty-one seconds) was a little slower. However, I was still on pace for my goal. "Pick it up and relax," I told myself. I approached the final quarter mile hoping that I was still on pace for the record. "3:02" "Heck, I relaxed too much," I thought. "I need to really bring it home," was all I could think.

It was just me and the track now. I was oblivious to my surroundings and heard nothing as I focused on relaxing and running hard for the last two laps of the race. My acceleration felt good and when I hit the tape I knew I had done something special. Moments later I heard the announcement over the P.A. system. "4:01.7... A new field house record!" I was ecstatic—but deep down knew that for a split second I had relaxed just enough to keep me from a sub-four minute mile.

"That was a great effort Jim," Coach Parks told me. "I've seen some fast times but never where someone did it all alone. If you had a pacesetter or someone to push you, I bet you would have run a couple seconds faster." It was comforting to know that although I no longer competed for the EMU Hurons, that I still had the support of my former coach and teammates. It made me reminisce about my first day on campus when I felt honored to be in the company of the legendary EMU distance stars whose names graced the record board.

Over the years, Coach Parks and I have remained good friends. He used my story as an inspiration to many, average, high-school recruits, convincing them that EMU provides a great setting for young men and women to make the most of themselves. If anyone ever asks me if they think Eastern Michigan University is a good choice, my answer is "Absolutely!"

My 4:01 mile resulted in a number of invitations to run and race against some of the best runners in the world that season. The indoor track circuit was followed by a spring season that included invitations to run the featured mile race at a number of prestigious track meets; including the Dogwood and Drake relays where I raced against distance legends such as Steve Scott, Eamonn Coghlan, Rod Dixon, and Mike Boit.

With no dependents, few bills, and some money in savings, I re-evaluated my goals and decided to head west to train for a sub-four-minute mile. The excellent weather and numerous high-quality track meets provided me with a setting where I could regularly train and race with many of the best distance runners in the world.

In the spring of 1980, I traveled to San Diego, California and slept on the couch of my former EMU teammate and then the current track coach at San Diego State University, Fred LaPlante. I searched for work half-heartedly knowing that the primary reason I was there was to train with a group of elite runners who would help me achieve my running goals. Fred introduced me to his roommate, 1:47 half-miler Brian Donahue, who along with Graeme Fell, an 8:25 steeplechaser from England welcomed me as their training partner. My plan was to work hard, run a number of off-distance races, and avoid the mile until I was ready to make a run at four minutes.

My workouts were encouraging as I felt myself making the progress I needed to compete with the best milers in the country. Fred helped me to plan workouts and map out a few races with the goal of improving my speed enough to reach my goal.   My target race was in late June at the California Relays in Modesto, California. Along the way, I ran a number of races turning in times of 1:50.2 for 880 yards and 13:36 for three miles, which boosted my confidence.

When I made my way to the track for the invitational mile in Modesto, I knew that I needed to stay focused and hang close to the leaders.   The star-studded field included several sub-four-minute milers including Steve Scott, Tom Byers, and world record holder John Walker. When I stretched and jogged during my warm-up routine, I glanced to the stands, recalling the enthusiasm, excitement, and energy I got from the crowd in the friendly confines of Bowen Field House in Ypsilanti, Michigan.   Something was missing when I looked up into the stands and saw strangers hovering around the Olympians, giving little notice to the kid from Ypsilanti.

I looked at my plain blue singlet and recalled how excited I was in the past when I put on my special EMU team jersey. My focus returned to the track and I headed to the starting line. My plan, much like in the past was to start quickly and to remain in contention as long as possible, reasoning that my chances of making up ground on these world class runners would be slim. As the gun sounded to start the race, I pushed myself to ensure I would be near the lead. I remained in close contact with the leaders for two laps but when a few runners made a move on lap three I lacked the acceleration and energy for a split second and a twenty-yard gap quickly opened. I reacted, trying to reel in the leaders to get back into contention however their last lap of fifty-four seconds had me falling back.

I ended up with a time of 4:04, good enough to win the majority of college and open races. However, in this field, it placed me near the back of the pack. With mixed feelings, I began my cool-down. I felt proud that I had given it a good effort, but felt that something was missing. I sat in the stands feeling the warmth of the sun and realized that what motivated me to enjoy racing wasn't the recognition and fame that came with running fast times, but the energy I got from the encouragement of my friends and family. I thought, "This was a good effort, but it wasn't fun." I questioned my motivation for my running goals and concluded that my image to others was not reason enough to want to run fast. How I felt about myself was what mattered most. During the ride back to San Diego, a feeling of peace and contentment came over me as I realized what was important to me.

Driven by this realization, I thanked my California friends for their support and hospitality, and returned home to Michigan. After six months of just running, I longed to renew relationships with long-time friends, co-workers, family, and the local running community. I looked forward to pursuing my professional career, strengthening my relationships, and running for enjoyment.

Running for enjoyment rather than being driven to win opened up a whole new world to me since I began to notice and enjoy my surroundings. I discovered value in the conversations and the time I spend with friends while running on the road. I remained somewhat competitive in local road races, however, was driven by enjoying the experience rather than pressuring myself to win. I felt at peace by striking the proper balance where my career could grow, I could run for the fun of it, and still have time to invest in my relationships with others.

****

"I'll be home at six. I teach water aerobics at eight-thirty, have four patients, and need to take Aunt Irene to the doctor. We can eat and then make it to our seven o'clock Bible study. Oh, and we'll have to drive separately because I promised to pick up April from work afterward."

This is a typical day in the life of my wife, Debbie. Despite her relentless schedule, she keeps a smile on her face which genuinely expresses her joy in doing all these activities. Her typical day would overwhelm most people; however she not only gets through each and every busy day, but embraces every minute of it.

A few years ago when her father was sick, she happily made the sixty-mile round-trip to his home saying, "Where would I rather be, these are my parents." Deb is an elite masters half marathoner and has mastered the skill of balancing work, family, marriage, church, friends, and more. Despite her busy schedule, running has become an enjoyable part of her daily routine. "I don't view it as a chore commitment. My runs give me energy. They are that quiet part of the day that gives me time to relax and reflect. My runs are fun." Deb has taught my children, me, and our friends that the key to happiness is all about having the right attitude and embracing and enjoying all that you do. Over the years, she managed to find time to keep a full-time career as an Occupational Therapist, raise our three children, arrange social gatherings with friends and family, participate in church and community activities, teach water aerobics, and run competitively.

To a lesser extent, I have learned from the busy demands of my years in college that time management and properly balancing the demands of your life will help you not only get through most anything, but enable you to enjoy what you're doing along the way. I've learned to joyfully fit in my morning run at six o'clock in the dark. I've also discovered that fixing my neighbor's door, or visiting my mother or aunt are not chores or obligations, but great opportunities to spend time with them.

Sometimes, however, I need a break. I discovered that an occasional total downtime to refresh and reload really helps. My wife and I plan an annual winter getaway trip where we do nothing but enjoy each other's company. Each summer, we plan time for our immediate family to travel to events and destinations. Along the way are a few long weekends or mid-week excursions.

A couple of weeks ago, my wife asked some friends over for a card game. "I don't think so," her friend replied in a reluctant voice. "I just had to take my daughter to school in Grand Rapids and we're exhausted from the trip."

"Oh I love that town," replied my wife. "Why just yesterday we took Rose to school and had a wonderful day. We watched her run, went to the park, had dinner, and met her friends. Most importantly we got to spend time with her."

"That sounds exhausting." Her friend replied.

"No, it was great... we enjoyed every moment. There is nowhere else we would rather have been." This attitude has taught me that embracing, rather than dreading, a busy schedule and enjoying the multitude of resulting experiences leads to contentment rather than a sense of being overwhelmed.

"Dad, can you let out the dogs today?" asked my daughter Renee. She was at the office until five o'clock, then was meeting her husband Greg for dinner, followed by her Greater Detroit Marketing Club meeting at seven o'clock. Renee displays many of the characteristics of my wife as evidenced by her joyful attitude regarding her active schedule. In addition to her full-time job as a Marketing Analyst, Renee is engaged in many activities including completing her master's degree; volunteering as a board member for the VegMichigan Foundation; participating in the Southeast Michigan Marketing group; belonging to a Bible study group; instructing a weekly yoga class and instructing a weekly water aerobics class. In addition, she has found time to move into and update a new home, run several times a week, participate in flag football, and spend time with family and friends.

What is the key to their ability to manage such an ongoing busy schedule? They have an attitude that is based on doing things for God and putting others first. The lack of focus on themselves gives them comfort in all that they do, knowing that God will provide for them. *"Do nothing out of selfish ambition or conceit, but in humility, count others more significant than yourselves. Let each of you look not only to his own interests, but also to the interests of others. Do all things without grumbling or disputing, that you may be blameless and innocent, children of God without blemish in the midst of a crooked and twisted generation, among whom you shine as lights in the world, holding fast to the word of life." Philippians 2:3-4, 14-16.* Putting God first and others before themselves has provided my wife and daughter with the strength to balance the demands and activities of the world with the mission of living for Christ by merging the two rather than searching for additional time to obey our God.

The worldly demands placed upon each of us can be overwhelming. The world has become more complex and it can be challenging to address all of your obligations and still have quality time in your life. The secret to ensuring you get the most out of your time is to embrace all of these demands with a positive attitude. This often requires assessing your daily routine and prioritizing what is most important. You will learn that depending upon God to take care of the important things in your life can help you by providing the support you need. Incorporating a Christian attitude, one that puts God first, and the needs of others ahead of your own, should be a key factor in your approach to doing everything. To have the proper balance and get the best results, you need to learn to give up the desire to control things by incorporating your daily time with God into all that you do.

Chapter Eight

Getting through difficult times – when things don't go as planned

"But as servants of God we commend ourselves in every way: by great endurance, in afflictions, hardships, calamities, beatings, imprisonment, riots, labors, sleepless nights, hunger;"
2 Corinthians 6:4:5

It was a Thursday evening in March of 1976 and I was jogging home from the Bowen Fieldhouse track. I had completed a few easy quarter-mile and 220-yard repeats, just what I needed to prepare myself for tomorrow's race. Tomorrow night I would be competing in what would be the biggest race of my college career:

the preliminaries of the one-mile run at the NCAA Track and Field Championships in Detroit. I started my workout late due to additional classwork and as I was heading home, the sun just sunk below the horizon, dimmed the evening sky and made it difficult to see. I took a short-cut across the field behind the track. When I descended the hill along the backside of the woods, my mind was focused on my upcoming challenge.   A few seconds later I was on the ground and into the street with noticeable pain in my left ankle.

I missed a step and tripped on the curb which caused me to fall hard. I slowly got up and tried to walk it off, but the throbbing pain was too much to take. "Loosen up," I pleaded to my body as I attempted to restart my jog. It was no use.   My leg gave way and I grimaced in pain. I walked instead and along the way tried in vain to run a few steps on the way back to my apartment.   I spent the night and a good part of the next day alternating ice baths and heat treatments and popping ibuprofen to no avail.

The race was at seven o'clock in the evening and the bus ride from Ypsilanti to Cobo Arena in Detroit was boarding at four o'clock.   I arrived at the bus with my ankle heavily taped and the hope that things would somehow be all right. I reluctantly approached Coach Parks, advising him of my plight. "Coach," I said. "I need to try to run this race.   It hurts like heck, but I can't miss this once-in-a-lifetime opportunity." I sat quietly during the forty-minute ride from Ypsilanti to downtown Detroit hoping and praying that somehow, someway I would be okay. I started my warm-up routine a little early hoping that I could find a way to land my foot to limit the pain.   As the beginning of the race neared, I convinced myself to get to the starting line and just run, regardless of the pain. I glimpsed hope when I attempted a few wind sprints from the starting line. I noticed significantly less pain when sprinting than when jogging. I looked up as the starter gave us the final instructions. "You need to stay in your lane until the far side of the track. Then you can cut in after the flag. You need a full body length to cut in or you will be disqualified. Remember gentlemen, the top two in this heat advance to the finals tomorrow." The excitement had let me momentarily forget about my sore ankle. I knew that I had to outrun a number of runners who had posted much faster times than me to get here. My strategy was to "get to the lead and hold them off." In many preliminary high caliber fields such as this, there was a strong likelihood that the best runners would run just fast enough to qualify, using their strong finishing kicks to make the finals with the least amount of effort. This would leave them with energy for tomorrow's finals. My best shot was to dictate the pace and then get the jump on them before they start their final kick.

I started fast at the sound of the gun. The pain in my ankle was a mere annoyance. I focused on beating the other eight runners to the turn. To my delight, I found myself in the lead as we rounded the first turn and cut to the inside lane of the track. I learned from my past experiences on a small board track, that passing takes extra effort and if I wanted the lead I would have to really work for it. I passed the 440 and remained in the lead. I sensed that the strong support from the hometown crowd came from my Eastern Michigan University uniform. I remembered from prior races that all it would take is a momentary lapse in concentration and I would lose the lead and my shot at the finals.

I continued to set a fast, honest pace, passing the half mile in 2:02. "These guys can think about tomorrow, but tonight is my big race," I reminded myself. We rounded the turn at the end of lap eight and my plan for a strong finish went into action. I surprised the field by accelerating and opened a ten-yard lead on the field. "Keep it going. Keep it going!!" I reminded myself. At any moment, I expected to hear the rumble of this elite field bearing down on me. The seconds passed as I remained in the lead, but I could sense a group of three runners on my shoulder as we entered lap ten. My legs and arms felt strong as I worked to hold them off by pushing myself to run hard around the turns. "They not only need to run faster than me, they need to run further if I can make them try around the turns." I entered the bell lap and reached deeper but could not hold off the challenge of 3:52-miler Wilson Waigwa, an elite Kenyan runner who was competing for the University of Texas, El Paso. When he passed, I focused my eyes on his back and gave it all I had! We rounded the final turn and I held my position and made sure to run through the tape to earn my spot in the finals. A few minutes later, I began my cool-down jog however my foot collapsed under me. The adrenalin from the race helped me to block the pain and temporarily forget about my sprained ankle.

This was only one of multiple episodes where I learned that unexpected events would continue to impact my ability to run. Despite logging in excess of 110,000 lifetime miles, I have spent more than my share of time on the sidelines or recovering from various setbacks and injuries. For the majority of my life, my nemesis has been Achilles tendinitis. I recall sitting on the sidelines or suffering through painful runs with the usual injuries that result from extending my body past its limits including chronic Achilles tendinitis, pulled calf muscles, pulled hamstrings, broken bones, back problems, and illnesses.

I have contributed a great deal to the bottom-line of companies that offer pain-relief remedies including analgesics, orthotics, athletic tape, braces, bands, cold packs, hot packs, ibuprofen, naproxen, and numerous other remedies. I have spent hours clutching a towel in pain as I immersed my foot into freezing cold ice baths. I have incorporated whirlpools, massages, yoga, and stretching into my daily routines. However the most effective remedy for the majority of these conditions was ten days of no running. Despite the barriers I have encountered, I continue to head out the door to pursue my passion. When in doubt I ask myself the question "Is it worth it?" The answer is always the same... "YES."

****

At work one morning, I noticed a group of co-workers standing around the coffee pot in our company's break room. "Hi Jim," shouted one of them. I approached the group and realized they were in the midst of a conversation about a top-rated television show that aired the past night. The show's theme revolved around comical situations of a number of unmarried young adults who regularly engage in casual sex, drink in excess and exhibit what I have learned to be immoral and unacceptable behavior. I voiced my concern that this theme like that of many of today's popular shows has de-sensitized society to the point where immoral behavior is acceptable. "Lighten up was their reply... it's only a TV show."

This encounter reinforced my thoughts about how modern society has become desensitized to what was once viewed as unacceptable behavior. The moral standard for content of entertainment such as television shows, music, and movies seemed much higher during past generations before freedom of speech became used as an excuse for allowing almost anything from entertainers to be publicly acceptable. Much of today's entertainment has turned to themes of shock and outrageous behavior to attract viewers and turn a profit. On the surface, it may seem harmless to compromise our morals slightly for such a trivial activity as enjoying a popular television program or movie that contradicts our beliefs. We can easily justify it because "everyone else does it." But where does this type of thinking often lead us? Is it ok to cheat on our taxes, drink in excess, gossip, stretch the truth, or hurt others for our gain?

As a society, our children and peers have learned to justify and accept immoral and sinful behavior since it has become commonplace around us. It's no wonder that the majority of young couples today choose to cohabit outside of marriage, that the divorce rate in our country has skyrocketed, and that drug use and crime have become epidemics across our country. Television ads, the internet, magazines, and billboards remind us that regardless of our resources if we want something, we deserve it and we should put ourselves ahead of others. Quite a contrast to what the Bible tells us in *Philippians 2:3-4. "Do nothing out of selfish ambition or vain conceit. Rather, in humility value others above yourselves, not looking to your own interests but each of you to the interests of the others."*

In the workforce, we are taught that success can be gained by working hard and climbing the corporate ladder. Society tells us if we continue to advance and achieve things in this world, we will gain contentment. The Bible teaches us that God requires us to work hard, however much of society has lost sight that motivation needs to come from pleasing Him and not for our personal pride. Pride can be a dangerous thing as it increases the potential for us to become focused on seeking worldly things, false idols and put our personal image ahead of God and others. And Jesus said to his disciples, *"Truly, I say to you, only with difficulty will a rich person enter the kingdom of heaven. Again I tell you, it is easier for a camel to go through the eye of a needle than for a rich person to enter the kingdom of God." Matthew 19:23-24*

Throughout history, greed and the pursuit of worldly power have caused devastation to many. The slaughter of people, mass hunger, and worldwide suffering has occurred for centuries as a result of individuals stopping at nothing to gain worldly power. More recently, the horrors of human trafficking, unethical practices to deplete employee pensions, insurance fraud, political bribes, and uncontrolled health care costs are affecting all of us.

The permissive attitude that prevails in our society demands that we regularly evaluate how we react to the moral dilemmas and challenges we are faced with. As a youth sports coach, I have witnessed the pressure put on young children by their parents to gain status through success in sports firsthand. Nowadays it is common for children as young as seven years old to be forced into private lessons, practice a sport year round, and then be publically ostracized by their parents when they have a poor game or don't make the team. This is a far cry from the enjoyment I experienced as a child through pick-up games with little parental guidance. The message our children may get from this type of pressure is- "I need to do anything I can to be the best, even if it is unethical or dishonest." When fifty major league baseball players were caught and penalized for using performance enhancing drugs, more than half of the fans interviewed commented, "Too bad they got caught"; rather than, "They had an unfair advantage and need to suffer the consequences."

Studying the Word of God and developing a relationship with Jesus Christ provided me with strength to recognize right from wrong and take the proper path when confronted with a difficult situation. My human nature resulted in a few falls and regrets but guided me to do the right thing more often than not. I continue to pray and ask God to help me make the choice that will best serve Him as I encounter roadblocks in my walk with God. Learning to live for God and put others needs ahead of mine has provided me with a sense of comfort as I strive for eternal happiness with my Father. As a youth coach, I stand by the principle that sportsmanship, teamwork, participation, and skills development come before winning and recognition and attempt to instill these ideas in the youngsters that I work with. As a father and role model, I remind myself that my pride can be a barrier to the development of strong relationships in my family.

To gain perspective and deal with the shortcomings in your life, you must accept that the world is imperfect and filled with temptation. Temptation coupled with man's' sinful human nature makes a difficult path to pleasing our Father and attain your quest for eternal happiness. What makes this more difficult is that these roadblocks are often disguised in the form of acceptable society behaviors, self-pride, good feelings, and a sense of personal triumph. It is easy at first to justify bending the rules. However, this behavior can often become a habit and over time blur the realities of what is right and wrong. Much like in a marriage, where a commitment is needed during good times and bad, you need to be prepared to deal with setbacks as much as accomplishments. In running and spiritual maturity you will surely encounter roadblocks and barriers to your plan that must be overcome to continue your quest. As a runner, you will undoubtedly encounter injuries, personal and professional conflicts, weather, and health issues that will require you to tweak your plan toward reaching your goals. Distractions, a busy schedule, peer group pressure, temptation, and motivation are issues that must be dealt with to keep on track toward fulfillment of your spiritual goals.

Chapter Nine

Family Time

"By wisdom a house is built, and by understanding it is established."- Proverbs 24: 3

Since early in our marriage, my wife and I used running as an opportunity to spend quality time together.

Whether we are running during Milford Memories, The Detroit Marathon, Frankenmuth or a new local event, seeing the Deren family participate and celebrate has become a fixture throughout the running community. In our early years of marriage, Deb had accompanied me via bicycle on several training runs and eventually began to run and race. Our three daughters were treated to rides around the neighborhood as we got the most out of the baby jogger we purchased after the birth of my first daughter. As my children grew, they viewed running as something that was a normal part of our day, becoming quite surprised when they went out into the world and learned that most people over twenty don't run.

Debs' interest in running provided the both of us an opportunity to spend more quality time together. Running together gives us an opportunity to escape the everyday activities and obligations that consume our lives by providing us with quiet time for sharing our philosophies, stories, inner thoughts, and confiding our problems to one another. As we run, our friends and neighbors wave and greet us, having no idea that we are on a running date. That is how we approached our time together on the road. As we traverse the courses and roads in our community our conversations are similar to those we might share at a restaurant or across from one another at the dinner table, including discussion about children, family, work, or joys, and challenges. Before we know it, we are turning the corner to our street and ending our workout. "Thanks for the run," Deb would say.

"My pleasure, we need to do this again," I replied as our next date was set.

It was seven-forty-two on a Sunday morning in late April. I pulled off my sweatpants, touched my toes, and did a couple wind-sprints down the tree-lined road. There was a refreshing chill in the air as the sun peeked up over the horizon. Our family had entered the 2012 Toledo Marathon relay as a family team. Each team is comprised of five runners who run distances from five to six miles each to comprise the 26.2 mile distance. Careful planning is needed to get each runner to the various starting points along the course as well as ensure that after we finish our segment we have transportation to the end of the race. The logistics of dropping off and picking up runners was simplified as our daughter Rachel volunteered to handle the transportation needs. I predicted that my wife would run the first leg of the Toledo marathon relay in about forty-five minutes, so I made my way to the second exchange point preparing to run the six-mile second leg and waiting for her to arrive. I would be handing off the baton to my son-in-law Greg. Then we would take the van to the next relay point to transport my oldest daughter Renee to the beginning of her segment of the relay and pick up Greg. We would wrap up the race with my daughter Rose running the final leg where she would finish at the University of Toledo football field. As we picked up Renee at the end of her run, she entered the van and we made our way to the finish to cheer for our last runner. We turned into the University, found a parking spot, and lined up along the finish area and cheered loudly as the name "Team Deren" was announced as the second place family team. We congratulated each other and made our way to the refreshment tent for a well-deserved break.

As the snow melted and winter gave way to spring earlier that year, our family convened at our dining room table to plan our summertime activities. We decided on a couple of family relay events, a half marathon and a number of local running races as well as a week-long trip to Savannah, Georgia. "I didn't know this was a part of the deal," said Greg as we chatted about the family events we had been planning for the upcoming year. Running was something new to Greg as he quickly learned after his marriage to Renee is that is what the Deren family does. He's adapted pretty quickly to the exercise regimen that has become a big part of our lives. "He's young and a good athlete and will do just fine." I thought to myself as we compiled our list of events. Over the three years since joining the family, he has run a number of 5Ks and 10Ks, a couple half-marathons, a few marathon relays, and a toughmudder event. "Just do it and have fun" is the attitude of his wife, Renee.

I discovered this attitude in Renee a few years before as we both entered the Capital City Half Marathon in Lansing Michigan in the fall of 2009. "How's the training going?" I kept asking her as the race neared.

"I did five miles yesterday... I think I'm ready" was her reply. On race day, I crossed the finish line and began a walk/jog back along the course expecting to see the worst. To my surprise, Renee was well ahead of her planned pace and smiling as she approached the finish. "Woo-hoo!" she exclaimed as she crossed the finish line completing her first half-marathon. "That's why we do what we do." I thought to myself.   Despite our busy schedules, a priority in the Deren household is to spend a great deal of quality family time together.   In addition to holiday gatherings, camping trips, summer concerts, and planned excursions several outings revolve around road racing.

Competing in running events had become a big part of Deb and my life long before we had children. Once they were old enough to run, our children were left to decide if it was an activity that they wanted to pursue. Our parenting philosophy concerning extra- curricular activities has been to expose our children to a variety of options and let them decide what they wanted to pursue. We were careful not to push them and whatever their choice was, we have always been fully supportive. Each of the girls participated in middle-school cross-country but sought out a number of different activities during high-school and beyond. Renee continued to run track but also played basketball. Rachel turned to golf, bowling, and tennis, which she continued to play in college. And Rose played basketball and volleyball.

Over the past few years, Rachel has kept busy enjoying dance, Zumba, and beginning a career in Family Services. Renee runs for fun and fitness while Rose has made the transition from others sports to running Cross-Country and Track for Alma College.

It was New Year's Eve of 2001 and I was scanning the latest Guinness Book of World Records that was a Christmas gift in Debbie's sister's home. My sister-in-law Nancy had progressed from beginner to competitive runner using her baby-jogger as a means to maintain fitness and care for her children at the same time. Debbie and her sister have been best friends for life and for as long as I can remember enjoyed a variety of outdoor adventures together. "1:32." "That's the record for completing a half marathon while pushing a baby jogger. You can do this!" I encouraged my sister-in-law Nancy. "I'll run with you," chimed in Debbie, hoping to support her sister's effort. Nancy was encouraged by our support so we laid out a plan and picked a race where she would try for the record. The big day came later that spring where she shattered the old record by more than one minute.

Nancy began running during the 1990's and quickly caught the marathon bug finishing over one hundred marathons. She has consistently been near the front in her races. Her accomplishments include a sub-three-hour marathon as a master at Boston and now, a world-record that has been certified by the Guinness Book of World Records for pushing a stroller for a half-marathon. A while after Deb and Nancy began to race, their older sister Pat came down with marathon fever and is in the process of running a marathon in every state of the U.S. As Grand Masters, the three of them are consistent threats to win their age divisions and place high in races. But their competitive nature is not what motivates them most, rather it is the opportunity to share their experiences and spend time with one another. Their time together is not a typical girls' weekend but focuses on sharing good times and camaraderie that revolves around marathon adventure trips. For them, finding a race that fits into their schedules is an excuse to spend quality family time together. On occasion, the group is extended to include the rest of our families as several of their children and close friends, like our children and friends, have taken up running as a hobby. Encouraged by our family lifestyles, Nancy's son Joe progressed in high school to earn all-state honors in the one-mile run and cross-country while their daughter Jacqueline has become an outstanding runner as a high-school freshman. This past summer, Deb's nephew Ryan trained and completed the grueling Grand Island Marathon in Northern Michigan, spurred on by the rest of the family.

For years, my wife and I competed in the Detroit half-marathon or marathon and saw an opportunity to share our good times with my sister and niece, Joan and Jennifer, who had recently started jogging by entering the 2010 Detroit Marathon as a relay team. Until now, they had never experienced the excitement and energy of a big running event. We were on our way home from the pre-race expo on the eve of the event and stopped to visit my mom. We had made and were wearing matching red shirts that sported a running logo labeled "Josie's Joggers" in her honor. "How do we look mom?" My mom was speechless. The gesture of running in her honor touched her heart.

The following morning, I was elated to see the excitement and nervousness of my sister Joan and my niece, Jennifer. Our relay team of Debbie, Rose, and I picked them up and we left their home in Walled Lake at five o'clock in the morning, when the world was dark and quiet. We saw a few cars along the way to downtown and as we approached the lights of the city, they got a glimpse of a bustling downtown Detroit they had never seen before, crowded with thousands of excited runners. We parked on Woodward and were greeted by the sight of 20,000 runners, 20,000 spectators, and numerous volunteers. The excitement of the runners and the event made such an impression on them that they became instantly hooked on running. Seeing the sun rise while crossing the Ambassador Bridge into Canada, running through the mile-long Detroit-Windsor tunnel, circling Belle Isle, and joining hands with my daughter Rose as we entered Ford Field into the finish, all to the roar of supporting fans did the trick. Since then, Jennifer has trained for and completed a marathon, and my sister, Joan has incorporated running, biking, and yoga into her daily routine.

Earlier that summer our family had made the quick trip to Milford, Michigan to run the Milford Memories 10K event. As we sat on the lawn in downtown Milford awaiting the awards ceremony, a fellow running friend said to me "You are a lucky man to have such a close family." I thought to myself "I know."

****

These are my children, their spouses, and my grandchildren. The look on mom's face, as she introduced her family to her friend Irene, was priceless. Mom had invited the family to a dinner sponsored by her church's women's club during the summer of 2008. The fact that the Deren family occupied four of the approximately twenty tables at the event, gave my mom a great sense of pride. Driven by the migration of the population of Detroit from the city into the suburbs since the 1960's, this neighborhood where I grew up has seen a dramatic drop in population. Forty years ago, the same function would have drawn well over 200 families. Despite the changes that transformed this once bustling neighborhood to a shadow of its former self, my mom, and her friends remained a close-knit group that were loyal to each other, their community, and their church.   This neighborhood was where these women spent the entire adult lives, raising their families, shopping, and worshipping. This was their home.   Strong family ties are a key characteristic of these people who live in this West-side Detroit community known as Warrendale.

The women of the St. Peter and Paul church ladies club experienced the most enjoyment in knowing they did their best to raise honest, hard- working, successful, and ethical children by putting the needs of others first. My mothers' example helped me to understand the Bible message from *Romans 13:8.* *"Owe no one anything, except to love each other, for the one who loves another has fulfilled the law."* When I watched my mom introduce her family to her friends, I could feel the sense of pride and contentment knowing we all valued the ethics and principles she laid out for us as children.

A few summers after that dinner, our family gathered in my mom's hospital room, acknowledging the realization she was leaving us soon. Despite being healthy for the first 80 years of her life, she had developed a heart conditioned that was causing her health to rapidly deteriorate. After a few months of heavy medication and numerous medical procedures, she decided to forgo further life-support treatments, knowing she had few days left on this earth. Despite the pain that came from her condition, the look on her face was full of joy, contentment, and peace. She knew she had lived her life putting God and others ahead of herself. It was the same priceless look she had on the day she introduced her family at the church dinner. Since her passing, holidays and anniversaries continue to be a joyous occasion as we remember her by knowing that she treasured family togetherness and obedience to God.

That same year, at my oldest daughter Renee's, wedding I felt a similar sense of pride realizing that my wife and I have raised three beautiful daughters who are obedient to God and depict the same selfless attitude that my mother had lived her life by. I stood in the church foyer I could hear the piano version of my daughters' music selection of "Love Story" by Taylor Swift coming from the next room. The smile on Renee's face said it all- she was ready and excited to begin the next chapter of her life... moving from my little girl to a married woman. When we walked down the aisle, I glanced at the congregation of family members and friends, all there to join in the celebration of her big day. I glanced toward the altar and spotted my wife whose beautiful smile echoed what was in my heart. Next to her stood Renee's best friends in the world, her sisters Rachel and Rose who for the first time appeared to me as beautiful young adults rather than my little girls.

Deb and I were thrilled when Renee purchased her first home just two miles down the road from us. However, we were more thrilled when she made the decision to wait until her wedding day to move in and begin her life with Greg. It must have been difficult to stand her ground and not succumb to the peer-group pressure of her generation that justifies relaxed morals. As I stood at the altar, I reflected on her journey to adulthood.

I thought back to a time when Renee and Rachel were young children. "Hi Dad, we're building a fort," came a voice from the living room. I walked in the door at the end of my workday, surprised to see Deb, Renee, and Rachel stacking pillows and sheets throughout the room. Play time with our kids was something we cherished. Deb and I realized their youth would pass quickly which made us determined to take the time to be there for them and enjoy their company. As new parents, it took some work but we discovered the proper balance between setting rules, using authority and instilling a work ethic with playtime.

As the children grew, we worked around our busy schedules to be there for their school, athletic, spiritual, and recreational events. We were quick to encourage and slow to demand that our daughters participate and excel in their activities. Giving them adequate space while being there for them, resulted in much joy and success for all of us. This philosophy allowed them to pursue activities that matched each of their unique personalities with enthusiasm.

Starting in the winter of 2001, I spent several years as a youth basketball coach for my daughter, Rose and several eight to twelve-year-old girls. I felt it important that the girls I mentored not only learn basketball skills but sportsmanship and respect for one another and their competitors. I loved the shirts that were given to coaches in our youth basketball league... "Professional Role Model," written across the chest. As parents, that is what we need to aspire to be at all times... a "Professional Role Model."

Several years later, Debbie, Rose and I were driving home from her high-school volleyball match. As we engaged in conversation, Rose said something that touched our hearts. "I'm really glad you're my parents." Her participation in high-school sports left an impact on her. She learned that many of her teammates' motivation came from negative pressure and an obligation to perform well to please their parents. She confided that some of her closest friends were regularly punished for not performing well in their sport. The experience helped us become better parents by ensuring that we encourage others through Christian-like actions.

Experiences such as these can help you to realize that through the gifts of marriage and family, you often find the support and inspiration needed to overcome life's challenges. Having consistent morals, values, and a strong commitment to each other is vital to having a strong and supportive marriage and family. The gift of marriage was given to us by God at the beginning of time as reflected in the Bible. *"But from the beginning of creation, God made them male and female. Therefore a man shall leave his father and mother and hold fast to his wife, and the two shall become one flesh. So they are no longer two but one flesh. What therefore God has joined together, let not man separate." Mark 10:6-9.*

Jesus Christ provided us with salvation by coming to earth as a member of the Holy Family where He respected and honored His mother and father. The Bible tells us a functional family unit that exhibits respect for one another is something valued by God. *"Children, obey your parents in the Lord, for this is right. Honor your father and mother, which is the first commandment with a promise, so that it may go well with you and that you may live long in the land. Fathers, do not provoke your children to anger, but bring them up in the discipline and instruction of the Lord." ~Ephesians 6:1-4*

A family that works together toward achieving a healthy lifestyle which stresses the importance of respect, compassion, well-being, and companionship can be a powerful thing. Deciding to raise a family results in major life changes as two people become responsible for establishing the foundation for a healthy mind and body of a child. Knowing the examples set by how you live effects the decisions made by your children provides strong motivation to live a healthy Christian life. The Bible teaches us that the physical family is the most important building-block to human society, and as such, it should be nurtured and protected. But more important, is the new creation God is making in Christ- the Church-which is comprised of a spiritual family who calls upon the Lord Jesus Christ as Savior.

Run To Faith

Chapter Ten

Becoming a Student – Never Stop Learning

"Behold, children are a heritage from the Lord, the fruit of the womb a reward." Psalms 127:3

A couple summers ago, I was inspired by the determination of my daughter Rose as she and her boyfriend Chris competed in the 2012 "Tri-For-Life" event. "I would love to try this, but I can't swim," I thought to myself. For as long as I could remember, I was convinced that swimming was not for me. Not only was I terrified of the water, I couldn't imagine learning a new activity at the age of fifty-nine. Still, I was intrigued. It was ironic that one of the things I was unable to help my children learn was how to swim. My daughters are all excellent swimmers, and along with my wife have all earned certification in lifeguarding. This has provided them opportunities for part-time jobs such as lifeguarding at the local pool or teaching water aerobics.

I loved to be in the water, but my usual spot was either in the shallow end or hanging on the edge of the pool. Due to the running injury, I sought out other activities to satisfy my workout habit. After weeks of urging I finally succumbed to Renee's request to participate in her deep-water aerobics class at the high-school fitness center. With the life ring around my waist I was confident I could keep afloat for the one-hour session that consisted of a variety of exercises such as running, kicking, pedaling, and stretching, all in water over my head.

After the class, I jumped in the open swim lane and made my first attempt to swim a length of the twenty-five yard pool. Head above the water and knees bent, I started out kicking and paddling but sank quickly. Renee held back the laughter and encouraged me to try some other activity such as biking in the park. The challenge of learning to swim was made. I headed to the pool early the next morning determined to figure out how to swim. "If seven and eight-year-olds can do this, so can I," I thought to myself. To stay afloat, I grabbed a kickboard, clutched it with both hands and by kicking my legs slowly, I made my way across the pool. Gradually I increased my distance adding a few moments of lowering my head into the water on each lap. After a few weeks, I was able to kick several lengths and was ready to try swimming without the floatation device. Determined to hit my goal of swimming one lap, I kicked hard and paddled my arms. After what seemed like an eternity, I neared the edge and immediately grabbed the wall gasping to catch my breath. I clung to the wall feeling like I had just run ten miles. "Now go back and do it again." I heard a voice say. I looked up and saw Rose's boyfriend, Chris, who is not only an excellent swimmer but also a coach of the Lakeland High School boys swim team and Penguins youth swim club.

The next lap seemed like an eternity as I struggled to make it. His critique of my form was humbling, but badly needed. "First of all forget everything you ever learned. The good news is you don't have deeply ingrained habits to break." His experience with first-time youngsters was just what I needed and he remained positive as he gave me some basic pointers. I leaned against the wall gasping from my lap and he taught me the basic mechanics of swimming. "You need to keep your body as flat as possible. Your legs are sinking because your head is up.

Rule #1... Put your head into the water and look down at the lane line. Drop your head into the water and just turn enough to get a breath of air. Don't gasp or hold your breath, just breathe normal and blow bubbles when your head is down." As much as I feared being under the water it made sense to me. I looked for an alternative but realized if I wanted to learn to swim properly, my face needed to be submerged. He had my attention.

"Rule #2..." he continued, "Make your body as long as possible. Don't kick from your knees but from your hips and reach for the wall with each stroke. Just work on those two things. Start slow and swim in the shallow end. If it feels good, go a length at a time... remember, if you practice bad habits you'll get good at bad habits."

For the next couple of weeks, I focused on keeping my head down and kicking from my hips. I swam one length at a time, working up from a couple intervals to ten, then fifteen, then twenty. Over the next several weeks, I gradually extended the length of my repetitions from twenty-five to a length of four hundred yards. It was time to move on, but I needed more help. I opened my eyes and ears seeking advice from experienced swimmers.

While resting between my swim laps, I noticed swimmers across the pool. I watched them closely and then attempted to mimic the fundamentals of their stroke. I was elated on Christmas morning as I opened my present, the book "Swimming for Beginners." I watched You-Tube videos applying new techniques as my training laps mounted. I gladly accepted advice and encouragement from my daughters as I worked toward my goal of learning to swim with ease and comfort and eventually enjoyment.

Recalling the path I took toward maturing as a runner, I felt the need to test myself to gauge my progress. I did some research and discovered a number of indoor triathlons are offered close to where I live. I was excited to learn the distances are typically much shorter than the outdoor lake events. These indoor events seemed to be a perfect place to start, so I entered and completed a few indoor sprint-triathlons. I thought about the swim often in the weeks leading up to each event. "What's the worst that can happen?" I thought. "If I get tired I can rest in the shallow end or hang on the lane line. Just get through the swim, even if you're last." On the bike, I would start out relaxed and gradually pick it up, confident I could hold my own. I had occasionally done some biking to maintain fitness while recovering from past running injuries. As a runner, I felt confident I could strongly bring it home as I had done hundreds of times before. I knew the swim leg would be my biggest challenge, but finishing it would also be my biggest accomplishment.

Throughout the weeks of swimming, I tried new stroke techniques—some taught by others, but most through trial and error. My confidence slowly grew as my fear of the water gradually subsided. Thinking ahead to the goal I had considered last summer,

I knew I needed to practice lake swimming, without a shallow end, lane markers and pool walls if I planned to compete in the "Tri-For-Life" in July. It is both convenient and coincidental that my home is situated on a small lake with very little boat traffic and close shorelines. I stepped onto the grass and felt nervous looking out into the lake when trying to plan my strategy and training course. I saw and felt wind and waves, weeds, sea creatures and the sun shining in my eyes, plus, I was certain my neighbors were talking about the crazy old guy in the red swim cap.

I decided my apprehension would reduce if I swam multiple loops between my neighbors raft and mine, which was a distance of about one hundred meters. "This is just four lengths of the pool." I reminded myself as I dove in. Over time, my comfort grew and I increased my distance and became familiar with lake swimming. After a few self-inflicted triathlon time-trials, I was ready for my race.

It was a warm, sunny morning in July as I made my way to the registration table for the 2013 Tri-For-Life in Otter Lake, Michigan. I was beaming with excitement as the race officials checked me in and painted the participant numbers on my arms and legs. I always thought it was cool to look like a triathlete with the competition tri shorts, painted on numbers, and fast-looking bike. I placed my bike on the rack in the transition area and carefully placed my helmet, towel, and running shoes where I could easily make the switch from swimmer to biker to runner. I felt a bit nervous as I lined up for pre-race instructions. Knowing I was one of the slower swimmers, I planned my strategy to wait for the crowd to enter the water and then take a position to the far right to avoid other swimmers that were heading for the first buoy. As the starting gun sounded, I took a deep breath and ran into the water as far as I could, making the transition to swimming as the water reached my neck. I felt relaxed as I headed toward the first marker, looking up occasionally to ensure I was still on course. At the first buoy, the course made a sharp turn to the left which I navigated perfectly. I felt good that I was ahead of a few swimmers as I swam past the second buoy which signaled the half-way point of the swim. As we neared the third buoy, we would make another left and head back to the beach. My relaxed attitude allowed me to stretch out my stroke and pass several more competitors. Fatigue settled in as I neared the beach, but knowing I was almost finished made the rest of the swim portion seem easy. As I made my way to shallow water and the shore, I stood up and ran to the transition for the bike portion of the event. I could hear encouragement from Debbie as I began the twelve and a half mile bike course. I quickly caught up to a pack of bikers and decided to hold their pace for the first six miles. As I neared the half-way point, I felt remarkably strong and decided to push the pace, leaving the pack behind. I worked the remaining hills and relaxed on the flat portions of the course, careful to save enough energy for the upcoming 5K run. Moving from the bike to the run was a new experience as my legs felt wobbly and kept telling me to stop. For a few minutes, I was reminded of the feeling I had in the last mile of a marathon. This was different though because as I continued to run my strength came back. The scenic out and back that ran through a nicely shaded area was a difficult but rewarding experience as I continued to pass a number of competitors. I turned the final corner and was elated to sprint to the finish line and complete my first sprint triathlon. Not only did I finish and feel good, I had earned a second place finish in my age group.

Thanks to the understanding, instruction, and encouragement I had received from my children and friends I was proud to wear my new "Tri-For-Life" t-shirt, a memento for having completed my first outdoor triathlon.

As a result of my accomplishment, I sought out new venues that would support my new interest in doing triathlons. I felt that improving my swimming discipline would make these events even more enjoyable. Recently, I enrolled in the Milford Masters Swim team. This group opened my world to new friendships and expert instruction. The patience, support, and expertise shown and by the coaches and others on the team has energized my desire to participate to honor God by being the best I can be. My progress and enjoyment while swimming changed my outlook. My initial goal was to swim well enough to participate in triathlons. However, I now swim regularly just for the fun of it.

While raising our family, I offered insights to teach my children many things about the sports they have tried. These insights include running tips, baseball skills, skills they gained through my role as their youth basketball coach, and most importantly good sportsmanship. As they have grown into adulthood, they have returned the favor by offering me insights into not only these sports but many additional activities. I have incorporated many of the things I learned in Renee's Yoga class into my stretching and strength-building routine. In addition to swimming, Rose has taught me some fundamental techniques taken from her basketball drills. I use Rachel as a mentor when hoping to learn a new dance step. The Bible instructs us to teach and learn from one another. *"You then, my child, be strengthened by the grace that is in Christ Jesus, and what you have heard from me in the presence of many witnesses entrust to faithful men who will be able to teach others also." 2 Timothy 2:1-2.* The key to learning from others is keeping an open mind and acknowledging that you can learn from them.

****

It was one o'clock in the morning on a winter night in 2005 and I was on my way to pick up my daughter Renee from the airport. As a high-school junior, she was returning from a church organized mission trip to aid workers and campers at Rancho Sordo

Mudo, a school for hearing-impaired children just outside of Ensenada, Mexico. We learned of the mission a few months earlier when our church hosted Luke Everett. Luke told the story of how he and his family sold their business and traveled to Mexico to dedicate their lives to helping hearing impaired children. The school was founded by his parents Ed and Margaret Everett who were introduced to the problems of the hearing impaired when Luke, lost 85% of his hearing from a series of illnesses at the age of five. As a result, they learned sign language and Margaret became an interpreter and teacher.

During a trip to visit missionaries in Mexico, they learned there was nothing being done educationally or spiritually to fill the needs of the poor and orphaned hearing impaired children in Mexico. So, the Everett's sold their home and business in North Carolina and went to Mexico as Faith Missionaries. The culture in Mexico provides little support for the disabled. The chances of these children being cared for to live a productive life were slim without this type of help. The mission has been widely successful as several children who entered the program as youngsters have developed the skills needed to live productive lives.

Inspired by their dedication, a group of teens and adults from Grace Church organized a mission trip to help support the ministry. On our ride home from the airport, Renee was enthusiastically telling me about her experience. "We built a new dormitory that will house ten additional children and worked on refurbishing the gymnasium. I worked in the kitchen providing meals and snacks to the workers and residents. We worked right alongside the residents who eagerly helped us in our mission. My favorite time was right after dinner when we studied passages from the Bible and engaged in group discussions." She barely paused for a breath. "What I learned most, is that no matter how many times I fail in my religious journey that God will forgive me. He loves me. All that is required is I truly believe Jesus Christ died for my sins and

I have faith in His promise of eternal life. Pleasing Him by living a Christian life as He taught us in the Bible is how we can show our gratitude. " The words and enthusiasm impacted me deeply as I have reflected on her insights many times since then and continue to work toward understanding my purpose on earth. "Just Believe and honor Him," has become a keystone to how I live my life.

In subsequent years, Rachel and Rose enjoyed similar experiences as they volunteered to help those in need through similar outings in places as far away as Trinidad and as close as our own neighborhood. Their faith has inspired us as a family to use their experiences in practical situations by living our lives in gratitude for Christ's sacrifice. I have seen my daughters make difficult decisions when confronted with the pressures of growing up. They have chosen to pursue friendships with people who have similar moral standards and continue to strengthen their faith through their own small groups of friends.

The members of our church congregation support our families' goal of helping others to please the Lord. Through the efforts of our small church group, we organized a picnic for our neighbors in the mobile-home community adjacent to our church property. The picnic was the idea of a young church group leader to build relationships with residents of the park. The initial outing during the summer of 2010 seemed to serve its purpose as we fed over two hundred families that evening. The event also acted as a springboard toward beginning a Bible study at the park. Over the past four years, this Bible study has been regularly attended by approximately a dozen residents and a number of church members.

The communication style of our group leader, Todd, has been well received as it has helped us to attain our goal of building strong relationships and lasting friendships through group activities and meaningful discussions. Todd has a knack for steering the conversations and direction so that the messages of our study are easily understood and applied to real-life situations. Regardless of the age, financial, or social status, each member provides insights that have strengthened our faith in Christ and desire to serve one another.

As a result, our family dinner table has become a forum for serious discussions about dealing with our thoughts and problems in a Christian manner. In contrast to my life as a youngster where questioning authority was discouraged and frowned upon, we often ask one another for opinions on how to deal with difficult situations in a manner that would please God. It gives me great pleasure to provide my point of view or turn to my family for comfort and understanding through difficult situations. Despite the rampant immorality, crimes, and sin in the world, my children, and their friends give me comfort in knowing that God's plan will be carried out and spread through the generation that we are raising. Not only do they provide a support system for their peers and friends, but for their elders and well. The Bible instructs each and every one of us to spread God's message and to teach one another. *"A disciple is not above his teacher, but everyone when he is fully trained will be like his teacher." Luke 6:40.* Our eyes and ears must be open to learning from one another.

The result of parental hard work can become a true joy later in life as your children grow to share their talents and help you continue your commitment toward a healthy physical and spiritual life. As your children have grown through adolescence and adulthood, you can take comfort in the knowing that they have matured as children of God. Your support system can be greatly expanded if you keep your heart open to learning from all people in God's world regardless of their age or background. You need to recognize and respect our God-given talents and those of all people around you to share life's experiences and your knowledge with others. As important as it is to utilize your talents as a teacher, it is equally important for you to be a good student. God made each of us in His image with our unique personalities and talents. So let us do as Jesus instructed us to and not bury our talents but share them with others. *"Well done, good and faithful servant. You have been faithful over a little; I will set you over much. Enter into the joy of your master." ~Matthew 25:21.*

Run To Faith

Chapter Eleven

Companionship and the Value of Groups

"Let each of us please his neighbor for his good, to build him up." ~Romans 15:2

Running down the wooded trail, my eyes focused keenly on the rocks and tree roots on the ground ahead of me. Deep concentration and awareness of my surroundings was important. However an occasional glance upward was needed to ensure I stayed on course. It was the summer of 2009 and I was running the 10th leg of the Dances with Dirt Trail Relay which was marked with occasional blue flags tied to trees. The ground became gradually softer and I soon discovered why this leg was labeled "The Stupid Lake." I survived the 2nd leg, a five-mile route known as "Mud Slide" which perfectly described the topography; plenty of hills and a long, muddy, downhill which was navigated by sitting down and sliding.

I turned left and got my answer to why this run was called "The Stupid Lake." The trail ended into a lake. My past experience of running this trail relay taught me to scan the landscape and locate the next flag rather than following the line of runners, who may or may not be on course. Scanning the shoreline, I noticed a few runners entering a path across the lake with the blue flag marking the course. After a few minutes of figuring out the best way to keep my balance and move as quickly as possible through the water, I decided to stay near the shore and run through the tall reeds. My strategy paid off as I glanced to the right to see other runners up to their head in water.

I re-entered the woods, soaking wet but refreshed and made my way through the final wooded mile to the exchange zone where I slapped the hand of my teammate Terry and he headed off to tackle the "Trail of Death." My teammate Dave greeted me with a dry towel and bottle of water as I cooled down and began my preparation for my next leg. Dave, Terry, Bob and I were the nucleus of our senior team that has competed in this event for the past seven years. Every year the course was adjusted with a few new surprises of mud, water, and hills along the 100K route. Our age and experience enabled us to regularly finish near the leaders of the pack as we were on our way to another top-5 finish and reward of free running shoes.

My introduction to trail relay racing began ten years earlier as my running partner and co-worker Terry introduced me to the three-day, two-hundred mile trail race across Northern Michigan known as the Great Lakes Relay. The Great Lakes Relay presents many challenges as the course traverses through forests, sand, abandoned railroad beds, two tracks, and country roads, however, is mild in comparison to the landscape of Dances With Dirt. It was at the Great Lakes Relay that I first met Dave Kanners. As we ran and chatted, I was awed by the experiences and adventures he accomplished. Dave turned to running after competing professionally as a performance-car drag-racer and then motorcycle racer. As a runner, Dave's craving for adventure meant he was always penciled in to run the muddiest and wettest legs on our relays. His resume of adventures included several marathons and several 50K and 100K ultra-marathons, including one at the North and South Poles. In between running adventures, Dave managed to bike solo across the United States twice and to climb to the highest peak in every state of the U.S. Race day, while we drove to the next leg of Dances with Dirt, he was sharing his plans for climbing Mount Aconcagua in South America.

As I got to know Dave better, we made plans to meet each other for running companionship and soon looked forward to our weekly runs with another teammate and friend, Bob Cross. Running from Dave's automotive repair business was always an adventure as we headed through the subdivisions toward the woods. "That's nothing... You should hear about the time that I... " was a phrase that inevitably would come from Dave sometime during every run. Bob and I joked about how some of the stories were outrageous and unbelievable; however the amazing thing we realized was that many of them were true.

Trail relays have become a good way for aging runners to continue to be competitive as handicaps for age and sex are factored into the results. Other than hitting retirement age, seldom will you find anyone over forty seeing an advantage to having another birthday; however this was one of those reasons. My teammate's desire to put together the perfect team consumed months of planning, calculations, and occasional bribes to attract elite grandmaster runners. They reasoned that a few youngsters with fresh legs were needed to take up a lion's share of the mileage, yet they needed to mix in the handicaps by recruiting older faster runners.

When recruiting team members, old and fast are good, but old, fast, and female is even better, making my wife, sister-in-law, and their friends prize catches. As each year passed, our ability to find ten healthy runners between the ages of fifty and seventy-five was difficult and our plans would often go awry when our prized seventy-year-olds would go lame a week before the event.

The races were fun, but the camaraderie of our training runs is where friendships were really built. Much as the training runs in college and later in life provided an escape from the pressures of school and growing up, these meetings provided rest and relaxation as we told stories, talked sports, and confided our problems and thoughts to one another.

During my life-long journey of running, I discovered that finding time to run required planning and flexibility.   When the children were young, I was fortunate to work in an environment that accommodated the majority of my core workouts during my lunch breaks.   When I traveled out of town for work, my routine included scanning the area for running paths before settling into my hotel.   Rather than be confined to a hotel, my desire to explore gave me an appreciation for the culture, history, and geography of such areas as: Steamboat Springs and Alamosa, Colorado; Washington DC; Orlando, Florida; Marietta, Ohio; and Manitowoc, Wisconsin.

As time went on, my circle of running friends and meeting places changed.   My count of close training partners continued to grow as I moved from the Ann Arbor to Plymouth to the Milford area and worked in Ypsilanti, Rochester Hills, Troy, and Pontiac. At each location, I sought out new routes, found new runners, and had new experiences. Probably the most consistent venue throughout my running life has been the eight-mile loop that circles Kensington Metro Park.   The course is both scenic and challenging as it meanders through hilly terrain alongside Kent Lake in western Oakland County, Michigan. On any weekend morning, I see familiar faces among the hundreds of runners who meet at the South parking lot and traverse the path around the lake. Kensington Metro Park is the home cross-country course for many high-school team meets, road races, and running groups gatherings. For the past ten years, my Saturday morning ritual has included a lap of the park with my running partner Terry and occasional other friends. We follow our run with breakfast at Leo's Coney Island.

I treasure the opportunities running gives me to meet and spend time with friends and family, yet I also find the solitude of occasionally running alone provides me great joy. Running solo gives me the opportunity to regroup and reset my priorities by slowing down the hectic pace of life. It is a time when I can clear my mind and just enjoy the sight of a sunrise, a blue sky, fall colors, or trees covered with snow. It is a time when I can listen to myself breathe, feel my arms and legs move, feel the wind on my face, and know that I am alive. Running heightens my senses which helps me deal with issues, calms my fears, and often clears my mind. I respect that running is not for everyone and as unique individuals we are free to choose activities that appeal to us. I understand activities such as swimming, playing basketball, walking, biking, music, and dance are preferred and better suited for many; however I know running is for me. The variety of running alone, in small groups, and at large events, in the forest, subdivision, or city, at night or in the morning all have contributed to maximizing my life's experiences and enjoyment.

****

Puppy, Palomino, Platypus, Pig, Possum. My mind raced as I jotted down as many animals names that began with "P" before the buzzer sounded. Our small group decided to play a quick game of

Scattergories after we prepared a dinner for one of the church families. Once a month, our Bible study group takes a break from analyzing scripture by spending time in a monthly "fun" or service night. In addition to our Sunday congregational service, Grace Church emphasizes participation in small groups as a key strategy for living a Christian life. My wife and I have found the weekly meetings reinforces the teachings and helps us apply key Christian messages to our daily lives.

Our current Tuesday night group is a particularly enjoyable and rewarding experience due to the outstanding energy of the youthful leadership, plus we genuinely support each other. The format works well for us as the discussions that revolve around key Bible passages are easy to understand and offer relevant perspectives from each member. The transformation from a traditional setting to a Bible-based congregation took a while for me to accept as it required me to think differently about worship. I was surrounded by people who worked hard at studying Gods' word and learned to trust one another enough to share deep personal feelings.

Saying that our first small group was "small" was a stretch, in that the membership included close to thirty members.   Prayers were intense, topics often very personal, and insights deep as we studied. For quite some time, I remained a quiet observer, offering little insights as I viewed, absorbed, and sorted out my feelings about the discussions. I sat in awe of others, respecting their outlooks and getting to know them better. Over time, these experiences taught me the importance of actively studying God's word and applying it to life's situations. The camaraderie that existed in these settings developed close relationships with others in the congregation, fueling my desire to learn and grow as a Christian. Our study of Bible lessons was complimented with bonding activities as well as community service.

We learned to help one another through a variety of activities including making meals for those in need, raking leaves for neighbors, working at the local food bank, repairing homes, and visiting the sick. I gained valuable insights about fulfilling my role as a Christian man through participation in Men's church retreats. Over the years, our mentors and friends helped me to overcome fears of speaking during the meetings, through learning to pray from the heart, simply and sincerely. This culture helped me develop a greater appreciation of the value of relationships. Most importantly, I learned to be bold in my faith by leading a Christian lifestyle and setting examples that would please God.   The Lord desires us to live together, supporting each other in harmony. *"Behold, how good and pleasant it is when brothers dwell in unity!" Psalm 133:1*

The small-group, church experience taught me about applying God's Word to many life experiences, thus transforming me from acting like a Christian to being a Christian. My newfound confidence gave me strength to deal with difficult situations in the workplace, in social events, and family events.   I learned patience, to think before I speak, compassion and caring, and to be non-judgmental in the interest of doing what is right in the eyes of Jesus.

Much like running, the camaraderie of small groups enhanced my spiritual life. Also, much like running, I value the personal time with the Father. I accept the strength and power of large congregational gatherings but am thankful for the support from the intimate relationships that small groups provide.

My time spent in the church group settings has given me a deeper appreciation for sharing my life with others. I thought about my appreciation of the relationships in my life while on a recent family vacation. In 2010, our family had taken a trip to Northern California to enjoy the wonderful sights and sounds of the mountains. I sat on the edge of the mountain looking over the majesty of the Yosemite Valley awed by the power and greatness of Gods' creation in nature.   As much as I enjoyed the moment, I realized that the experience was even better because my family was there to share it with me.

I also thought about how spending occasional time alone can be an important and rewarding experience. Great strength and pleasure can be derived from the quiet solitude experienced during the morning run on a perfect summer morning or the personal relationship and prayer we engage in with our Savior. It is important to realize that the joys and experiences we encounter during our lifetime are enhanced through meaningful relationships with others. By engaging with others, we develop lasting relationships and a strong support system which provides additional motivation. Group runs and participation in events are an excellent way to share our experiences and build lasting friendships. Likewise, small church groups help us to share, analyze, and support each other through group prayer, conversations, and activities.

Chapter Twelve

Giving Back

"Love one another with brotherly affection. Outdo one another in showing honor." ~Romans 12:10

A light rain fell when the final runners and walkers made their way to the 5K finish line. "I'll bet you that some hot oatmeal would taste good and warm you up about now," I mentioned to the teenage boys standing in the cool mist as they eyed the post-race refreshment table. Still recovering from my injury, I attended and volunteered at running events to keep alive my interest in the sport. Volunteering also gave me an opportunity to give something back to the running community that had supported my passion for the past forty years.

Through volunteering, I gained an appreciation for the effort, time commitment, coordination, and logistics required to put on a successful event. At my latest volunteer position, I turned the corner to the Commerce Township Municipal Offices and was greeted by more than eighty volunteers who had given up their Saturday on a November morning in 2013 to support the second annual "Outrun Hunger" event sponsored by Grace Church. The commitment and dedication of volunteers began months prior to the event. Committees were formed to handle advertising, route planning, parking, and to seek donations for food, other amenities and awards. The ultimate goal was to raise money to provide meals for needy families.

In 2012, Grace Church started "Outrun Hunger", a 5K fun-run race for charity, with the goal of raising enough money to feed one hundred families during the holidays. At that inaugural event, 100% of the race registrations went toward this goal. In addition, a number of local-area businesses donated time and services for the event. The results shattered race organizers expectations as over $9,000 was raised to support two, local food banks, enabling over 460 families to enjoy a hot meal at Thanksgiving or Christmas. Despite the effort and success of the event, these organizations in our area receive requests from approximately 1,345 families during the months of November and December.

There was a light mist in the air, but the fifty-degree temperature for a November morning in Commerce Township, Michigan was welcome. We were encouraged that many area residents braved the wet weather to participate and help raise money to feed our neighbors. As successful as the race was, the post-race survey gave us hope that we could look forward to continued support from those who participated.

It was encouraging to see the generosity of people who contributed their time and provided financial support for our community. This generosity is occurring across the country. In towns such as Elmhurst, Illinois; Stockton, California; Lawrence, Massachusetts; Sacramento, California; Dawsonville, Georgia and 100's more, running event such as "Outrun Hunger" raised thousands of dollars which are directed toward feeding the hungry of their communities.

Shortly after the millennium, I set a goal for a fall marathon and decided upon a race in mid-October of 2001. As I worked through my training schedule, I noticed a new event, a 30K race in nearby Milford, Michigan and thought it would be a good opportunity to simulate race conditions in preparation for the 26-miler a month later. The race was a memorable experience as it was a well-marked scenic, but challenging course that started and finished at a local restaurant and banquet facility. The post-race party included not only the usual amenities of bagels, bananas, granola bars, and Gatorade, but raffle prizes and live entertainment.

Our family socialized with other runners and spectators awaiting the posting of final results while we listened to the race director address the finishers and their families. "Thanks to your participation and generous donations, we have reached our goal of raising enough money to fund a new recreational bike path that will extend six miles from downtown Milford to Kensington Metro Park." "Wow, what a great idea," I thought. I've always been an advocate for more pedestrian friendly access throughout our community and this effort thrilled me. I looked around I noticed the hundreds of volunteers it took to organize and marshal the event. I noticed the number of local businesses that donated food, prizes, and their time. The commitment inspired me to support this effort by volunteering in subsequent years to park cars, marshal the course, or provide water to runners on the course. As the race had met its goal of building the trail, organizers have continued their support of the community through donations to local food banks, the area HOT (Heroes of Tomorrow) team, and local high-school running programs.

Throughout Michigan and across the United States, communities have called upon the generosity of runners, their friends, and families to fund incredible missions and make a difference in the lives of many. Whether it be running to raise funding and awareness for popular causes such as Multiple Sclerosis, Diabetes Education, Special Olympics, Breast Cancer, Heart Disease or special causes like feeding families, building trails, enhancing the community, or support local youth organizations; racing events are used as a tool to make a difference in the lives of many in need. In addition to the support provided through entry fees and donations, there is always a need to work behind the scenes as a volunteer and give back to the running community that makes your pastime possible.

****

During every second Saturday of May, my neighborhood is characterized by heavy traffic and people from the greater community scanning garages at our annual, subdivision garage sale. Although this is not one of my favorite activities, I often accompany my wife when she looks for useable used medical equipment for her home-care patients. As we scan the yards, our eyes are open to view certain items such as walkers, canes, crutches, and grab bars. As a home health, occupational therapist, Deb serves a predominantly elderly population in a variety of settings. Many of her patients are home-bound and immobile due to accidents, illness, disease, and aging. Many live their lives with limited family and financial resources. They have needs, but cannot afford the luxury of medical equipment that could give them some mobility and independence. Deb improves their standard of living with her thoughtful purchases.

Her approach taught me how small acts of kindness go a long way. "God Bless You," I heard from Elsa, an elderly woman standing in the doorway of her home. I repaired a hand railing on the porch of one of Deb's patient's homes and was preparing to paint it. A recent storm had dropped a tree onto her porch breaking her stair-rail in half. "Without the railing I can't get up and down the stairs. What can I give you for your time?" Elsa asked. The look of gratitude on her face was all the reward I needed as we chatted and I finished the job. "God Bless You," Elsa told me as I was preparing to leave.

I replied "God has provided me with the skills, strength, and beautiful weather I need to help someone like you." She smiled, agreed, and we instantly bonded.

Over the years, my wife's attitude of helping others has become more deeply ingrained in how I live my life. We installed grab bars in bathrooms, built a wheelchair ramp, fixed broken walls, hung doors, and fixed leaking pipes for those that could not. "You don't have to do this if you are busy," She always says.

"I love fixing things and working with tools. "I reply, knowing my underlying reason is helping others for that is what God instructs us as Christians to do.

I have seen and am deeply influenced by that same attitude of the leaders of our church. "Growing Christ-followers who are alive in Christ, connected to each other, and engaged with the world," is the mission of Grace Church. These words helped me grow as a Christian by instilling in me the need to interact with others to reap the benefits of my faith. My biggest revelation about being a Christian was when I realized that attending weekly church service and belonging to the Church as an active member are quite different. I realized a church is more than a physical location. It is comprised of a community of worshippers. Only then did my spiritual ideals become relevant in everything I did rather than just on Sunday morning.

Praying with others, performing community service, singing praise to God, and participating in Bible studies are some of the weekly activities available for me to engage with the church community in the interest of supporting our mission. Our community service includes dozens of church members volunteering for opportunities such as cleaning up a yard for a disabled woman so she would not get fined.

In my attempt to understand the value of our church family, it is apparent that our church leaders work hard to prepare messages, teach the congregation, spread the word of God, and organize events to reach out to the community. They do these things to work through the members to accomplish the mission set forth by Jesus Christ. Accomplishing their goals is fulfilled if the members are willing to give back to one another.

An important insight I gained in my Christian walk is to seek opportunities to do the right thing and use the situation to spread the message of Christ. When I meet new people and encounter strangers I don't have a way of knowing their spiritual outlook, so I keep my eyes open for opportunities to drop a hint just in case there is a situation where I can help to strengthen their faith.

I struggled for some time to heed God's command for us to spread His Word through evangelism, reasoning that grown people have had a lifetime to determine if they wanted to follow God's word and little that I say would have an impact. My small-group experience taught me people are often in difference places with their faith and sometimes a kindly push, for example, provides them the strength and support they need to grow spiritually. Past experiences taught me that loud and strong preaching more often than not alienates those we want to reach. So, instead, I seek a gentle way to create the opening. I start by seeking out friendships. Once the relationship is established, I work to build credibility through my actions as a role model and making the right choices. And finally I look for opportunities to allow these people to know I am a follower of Jesus Christ.

The opportunity to participate in many activities would not be possible if volunteers weren't there to make it happen. Across our country, running communities have played a key role in supporting efforts to make life better for those in need. Following the direction of Jesus Christ, church communities have worked to make the world a better place through their generosity and commitment to others. In our fallen world, it is impossible to address the needs of all who have experienced hardships. However, you can improve the lives of many by lending support in the form of your talents, time, and financial contributions. In addition to improving the standard of living of your neighbors, your contributions often provide morale and spiritual support. You need to do as Jesus instructed in the Sermon on the Mount. *"So whatever you wish that others would do to you, do also to them, for this is the Law and the Prophets."* ~*Matthew 7:12* Acts of kindness and generosity can have tremendous positive physical and spiritual impacts on others in the form of feeding the hungry, engaging the lonely, sheltering the homeless and saving lives both physically and spiritually.

Run To Faith   James Deren

Chapter Thirteen

Fueling Your Journey

"I am the living bread that came down from heaven. If anyone eats of this bread, he will live forever. And the bread that I will give for the life of the world is my flesh." ~John 6:51

I was thankful for the beautiful weather on an early June day in 2009, in the Huron-Manistee Forest in Northwest Michigan. In our fifth consecutive year of running the North Country Trail relay our team, "Not Yet Determined", had great expectations for breaking our streak of second-place finishes. Our captain, Terry had come up with the name with the hopes of one day hearing the announcer say "This year's winner is not yet determined." In prior years we had encountered rain, heat, and bitter cold temperatures; however the blue skies and mild conditions made this an ideal day to attack our goal of a victory.

The North Country Trail Relay is a challenging but beautiful route that requires five runners to traverse 77.6 miles of the North Country Trail between Mesick and Baldwin, Michigan. Unlike the novelties of swamps, rivers, lakes, and other off-trail barriers that characterize other relays, the North Country Relay is a sure-footed course.   Like many other relays, the race is handicapped to provide an equal opportunity regardless of gender or age.   Our team consistently finished near the top overall with our handicap placing us just one minute and fifteen seconds behind last years' champions, the "Onsted Ringers". This year was different than previous years as our senior runners came into the event injury-free and in decent shape. Our team captain, Terry added one young runner, Bob's son, Adam, who recently completed his college running career by earning all-conference honors at Miami University. We counted on Adam to take up the bulk of miles and most difficult legs.

When we approached the checkpoint for the 15th and final leg, I knew what I had to do. I put on a fresh t-shirt, clean socks, my trail shoes, and got out of the van to prepare myself for my run.

Legs tight and heavy, I jogged and worked up to a few strides trying desperately to summon enough energy to give our team a shot at the title. "You know what you need to do," Terry told me. "If Deb keeps us close you have a shot." I waited eagerly at the final exchange point ready to attack the trail.   The quiet of the forest was broken by the cheers of our competitors urging their runners on. I looked up and realized that my challenge would be difficult as our main competitors final runner was a fast twenty-five-year-old college runner.   "We expect Deb to come in about three minutes behind Onsted so you'll have to keep the gap no less than a minute per mile slower than him." Terry figured.   Much like any other relay, I didn't get involved in the pacing, results, or figuring handicaps, I just ran. Terry and Bob however spent hours studying the course, past performances, and calculating team handicaps. "Their last guy usually averages six-minute miles—so you'll have to run sevens. The course has three big hills however the last two miles are flat and fast. At three miles, you'll cross a road where you can check your time."

I quickly realized this would be no easy feat. Despite the variety of difficulty and terrain, a trail pace was about one minute per mile slower than road race pace. At fifty-five-years-old, I had not seen a six-minute-mile pace for quite some time. However, I prided myself in excelling on the trails and knew I had a shot.

As Onsted's final runner passed, Terry started his watch, hoping to see Deb within the next three minutes. Terry reminded me that our handicap though less than last years' team gave us an eight minute and thirty-second adjusted time advantage over our nearest competitor. As we waited for Deb with our slim hope still alive time seemed to stand still. "It should never have come to this." I thought to myself.

Just two hours earlier things had changed dramatically to put us in this spot. The race started promptly at six o'clock in the morning as the more than one hundred teams headed onto the 4.8-mile first leg of the course from a roadside park just outside Mesick Michigan. I was assigned legs one, five, and ten which would give me adequate recovery time to cover 13.1 miles, my allotment of miles in the relay. My experience taught me to hold back at the start and try to move up as the race developed. I was elated that during the first leg I navigated my way from the middle of the pack into spot number five as I tagged our fastest runner Adam. The move seemed to pay off as Adam attacked the hilly nine and a half mile second leg, finishing ahead of all of the competition. As the day progressed, and the distance between runners on the course lengthened, our team managed to stay near the front of the pack. By mid- afternoon, I realized I had rationed my energy wisely and refueled my body with adequate water, bananas, and energy gel leaving me eager to give it all I had on the 3.1-mile tenth leg.

Of the teams that remained near the lead, our handicap advantage left the Onsted team as our biggest threat. I started the tenth leg of the relay. I kept focused on working hard to build our advantage and was pleased to know I had gained two minutes on their runner. When Bob took off on the five-mile leg eleven, we held a five-minute lead. Knowing we had about forty minutes until the next leg, we enjoyed our leisurely ride on the vehicle route to the next checkpoint where our fastest runner Adam was sure to extend the lead even further. With two-thirds of the race complete we were confident and excited. We parked the van, walked to the exchange point and began the wait. The next twenty minutes seemed like an eternity as we patiently waited for Bob to come into view. When we saw the lead teams come through the checkpoint we expected Bob any moment, however, time continued to pass and we continued to wait. A few more teams including Onsted ran past and our fears that something had gone wrong were intensified.

In the past several years, we witnessed a number of runners taking a wrong turn and moving from contention to also-rans. Finally, we noticed the man with a blue singlet walking along the trail toward the exchange point. "Sorry guys, but about two miles back I pulled my hamstring. I tried to work it out and run but just couldn't." We were compassionate knowing that unexpected injuries were a risk of any fifty-year-old runner and reassured him that we understood. Before I could ask how far back we were, Terry had done some quick calculations and determined that our five-minute lead had become a five-minute deficit. "If we can make up two minutes on the last few legs we still have a shot," Terry exclaimed. The challenge was more complicated in that Bob was supposed to run the final leg. "Adam is running now and he'll make up some time. My leg will put me at fourteen miles and Deb runs next." Terry explained. After going over a number of options, I reluctantly volunteered to add the final five and a half miles that would give me a total of 18.6 miles of tough trail racing for the day. I was able to mentally prepare myself for another run but questioned my ability to regain enough energy to give us a shot.

My experience as an endurance athlete provided me with a basic understanding of how to fuel my body for training and competition. When I transitioned from the middle distances to longer distances, I quickly learned, mostly through trial and error, the importance of fueling my body appropriately to achieve maximum performance. Whether it was a marathon, long training run or 10K in the heat, I crashed enough times to seek a solution to the challenge of staying strong during my runs.

In the early days of distance running, up through the 1980s, the key to maximal performance was focused primarily on building an aerobic base plus mental toughness. More recent research has uncovered the equal importance of adequate rest and proper nutrition. Adding this dimension to an overall training program has resulted in significant improvements in endurance sport performance. The importance of a good nutrition plan for overall health is strongly linked to improved quality of life for endurance athletes and the average person.

To maximize performance for a single high-intensity activity such as distance running requires an understanding of how to quickly replenish your metabolism. For energy while running, the body uses a combination of proteins, carbohydrates, and fats. However, carbohydrates are the most efficient form of fuel available to burn. Carbohydrates are stored as sugar for an immediate release of energy. If the body runs low on carbohydrates, runners commonly experience hitting the wall. Many athletes carb-load before an event to prevent hitting the wall. In the past, carbohydrate loading was relegated to the night before the event to keep the runner from running with a full stomach. However, energy bars and gels have revolutionized the sport by providing easy-to-digest alternatives. These are ingested just prior to and during competition. The recommended use of an energy gel is fifteen minutes before starting a run and then every thirty to forty minutes during the run.

In addition to carbohydrates, I learned that proper hydration is essential to fuel my muscles. Many sports drinks replace water and electrolytes lost through sweating while running. Water is the best fluid replacement for activities less than sixty minutes in duration. Sports drinks are meant specifically for athletes to recharge the body's muscles with glycogen. This gives the body more endurance for long runs and helps to recover after workouts.

In my earlier years as a runner, I paid little attention to the science associated with maximizing my performance and maintaining overall fitness.

For many years, I convinced myself that as long as I burn more calories than I ingest, I would be able to maintain an ideal weight and be healthy. Much like many runners, I reasoned that my habit of exercise would give me permission to eat whatever I wanted and remain lean and healthy.

When I reached the age of fifty a few years ago, I opened a packet from my insurance company stating they required an annual physical. The physical included blood pressure, cholesterol, diabetes, body mass, and a nicotine test. Upon receiving the follow-up phone call, I was happy to hear most of my vital signs were excellent but astonished to find my total cholesterol was borderline high at about two hundred. The nurse explained the danger of high cholesterol that it restricts the flow of blood and could lead to a number of devastating illnesses including stroke, diabetes, and heart issues. The office staff agreed that my ideal weight, exercise regimen, non-smoking and non-drinking status and positive mental outlook led them to believe the cause was probably hereditary. The recommendation of cholesterol lowering medicine seemed like a good option as the most common side-effect included a slight chance of muscle weakness. After three months of medication, I was retested only to find no change in my health. Doubling the dose resulted in slightly lower cholesterol but brought along muscle weakness that negatively impacted my running.

I sat down and reviewed my options. Research revealed positive results had occurred in patients who greatly reduced their intake of fat. The diet recommended fulfillment of daily calorie intake by eating healthy foods such as broccoli, fish, green leafy vegetables, oranges, carrots, garlic, fiber, and oats. I made a three-month commitment to a healthier diet by removing soda, chips, ice cream, and white bread from my diet, as well as restricting my intake of red meat. I was anxious and curious when I received a call to learn the results of my next physical examination. The exam results showed a significant decrease of my total cholesterol to 170. I was elated to learn my lifestyle change was more effective than the alternative of being dependent upon medication for my health. Instead of celebrating with an unhealthy snack, I found my eating habits and desires had changed and gladly embraced my new lifestyle. To keep the momentum, I decided not to deprive myself of anything in particular but to make healthier choices when possible.

Adopting this lifestyle revealed how difficult society has made it for Americans to adopt good eating habits. We are bombarded with messages that correlate unhealthy food to fun and convenience. Fast food that is filled with empty fat-laden calories has become the norm for many Americans, leading to increasingly dangerous obesity rates. I recently walked into a restaurant for a coffee and was appalled to see my choices included large, larger, and huge... nowhere was there an option for a small or medium.

To maximize performance in sport, it is essential to provide your body with a diet that supports good health through proper nutrition. A training regimen that strengthens the body and mind through hard work and motivation only provides part of the ingredients needed for success. Without proper fuel and rest, the body will not rebuild and strengthen itself to reap the benefits of your hard work. As we age, it becomes even more important to make proper choices and slow the effects of time on our body, to live a long, healthy, and happy life. In youth, we often fall into the trap of thinking that a fitness regimen will allow us to eat whatever we want to maintain optimal health. However, invisible killers are at work if we take this approach. As we grow older, we understand that despite diligent workout habits, the effects of poor nutrition will eventually lead to chronic diseases such as poor circulation, high blood pressure, unhealthy cholesterol levels and weight gain. Over the past several years, many research studies have been done to enlighten us about the effects of poor nutrition choices. As a result, many articles, books, support groups, and experts have made this information available to all of us.

Fortunately, groups are forming to educate people about food content and to promote a healthy diet. In a recent book entitled "Blue Zones, Lessons For Living Longer from the People Who've Lived the Longest", Dan Buetner summarizes the common characteristics of people who live the longest and healthiest lives across the globe. I read with interest and quickly related to the nine guiding principles outlined in his book—in fact most of them applied to this day at the North Country Relay.

The trick for me is viewing food as fuel, not just something to address the hunger. Before my additional run on that June afternoon at the North Country Relay, I drank plenty of water, plus a little energy drink and ate a peanut-butter sandwich. I placed an energy gel in my pocket for later.

Deb approached and slapped my hand. Terry yelled, "Three minutes and two seconds... have a good run!"

At first, I was concerned about the tightness in my body; however within a few minutes I became relatively loose and settled into a comfortable pace. I was eager to attack the first hill, but went up at a moderate pace instead. I continued to stretch my legs into a pace that felt like a seven-minute- mile. I approached the road near three miles and looked at my watch hoping that I would be close to the seven-minute pace needed to give our team a shot. Deep down, I knew that I was doing the best I could, but how much of a toll did the prior sixteen miles take? "21:05." "Perfect," I thought to myself.

Past the road was the final steep incline. The excitement of knowing I was on pace gave me the energy to work the hill and then bring it home over that last two and a half miles. I continued to push the pace until I finally could hear the crowd in the distance. Deb and Terry greeted me as I headed across an opening in the path about a quarter mile from the finish. "It's going to be close," I heard them shout as they followed me toward the finish line. I spotted the finish banner and reminiscent of my college track days unleashed my final kick. As I crossed the line, I bent over in exhaustion and slowly made my way toward my teammates. "How did we do?" I inquired.

"We're seventh overall, but I'm not sure after handicap... It's really close," Terry said. "We'll have to wait for the final results."

I went to the van to get dry clothes and headed for the makeshift shower. Rejoining my teammates, we anxiously waited for the announcement. A few moments later the results were ready. "In the closest finish in race history, the winners of the 2008 North Country Trail Relay with an actual time of nine hours, forty-six minutes and fourteen seconds is 'Not Yet Determined.'" The handicapped time left us twenty-eight seconds ahead of the runner-up, Onsted Ringers. Elated, we enjoyed the moment knowing the combination of training, age, experience, toughness, and recovery had propelled us to the win. We quickly gave thanks and thoroughly enjoyed the post-race refreshments.

****

Improvements in my health resulting from a greater awareness of my eating habits have changed the way I view food. Instead of eating to alleviate hunger I find enjoyment in the taste of nutritious offerings. Our family was enjoying an outdoor dinner on our deck during the summer of 2011. I was pleasantly surprised by the wonderful flavor of the sweet corn we purchased at the local farmer's market. I enjoyed my dinner and thought about what it would be like to grow my own vegetables. I knew I could just as easily visit the local markets to purchase the foods I loved but started to wonder if I could care for a garden with the skills to grow my own food. I decided I would start small and try a few varieties that seemed easy to care for.

With rake and shovel in hand, I eagerly awaited the early spring so I could prepare the plot of land I had picked out. My research told me crops such as lettuce, snap peas, green beans, and radishes are relatively easy to grow, requiring a good amount of sunshine and adequate watering. My experiment continued as I searched for a spot that would give my crops a good amount of late afternoon sunshine. I decided on a small plot at the edge of the deck on the west side of my house. I engaged the staff at the local greenhouse to explain my goal and was enlightened with tips for growing my selection.

Year one was a learning experience as I quickly found that a fence was needed to ward off the rabbits and other wildlife. The animals feasted on my lettuce, and the sunlight proved to be inadequate for radishes, but my green beans and snap peas provided me with enough success to alter my plan and make some adjustments for the next summer.

As soon as the weather permitted, I marked off a much sunnier plot of level ground and began to expose the soil. Learning from the past year, I constructed a two-foot high fence around the perimeter, adding a gate and the recommended fertilizer. Throughout the year, I watched in earnest and diligently pulled weeds and watered the crops in my garden. The result was fantastic. I watched the beans, radishes, peas, lettuce, and turnips grow. By early fall, I added tomatoes and we were feasting on the bounty of our work.   During the winter months, I found myself diligently planning for next year's goal of expanding the crops and adding a number of new foods.

As we ate dinner one night, I thought to myself, "these green beans are delicious". I was beaming with joy as I realized the time I put into my summer garden resulted in a successful bounty of green beans that my family and I enjoyed during this past summer.

My desire to garden is supported through my visits to the library to learn to get better results, as well as conversations with friends and family who share my passion for growing their own vegetables. I have found great joy as a result of the planning, preparation, maintenance, harvesting, sharing, and eating activities associated with my newfound hobby. I can now call myself a gardener.

My passion for gardening followed a similar pattern to many of my other chosen activities. As a child, I spent a great deal of time participating and working to grow my skills in activities such as baseball and basketball. As I aged, I became interested in activities that included playing the guitar, running, golfing, bowling, repairing and updating my home, raising a family, updating my job skills, and most recently in coaching, swimming, hiking, traveling, and cycling.

My interest in each of these activities was initiated by first giving it a try. As I continued to participate, my desire to improve my skills involved surrounding myself with educated resources and situations. I sought out methods and avenues that provided me with practice time, knowledge, coaching, mentoring and the companionship of people with similar interests. Over the years, my interest in a number of the activities has waned. However my interest in new activities has grown. I recognize my environment was an important factor in the continued growth in these areas. During college, my interest in playing the guitar was high as long as I was surrounded by classmates who enjoyed music. After graduation, I lacked the support system needed for me to continue on my own and my interest slowly died. As a runner, I regularly sought out friends as training partners, subscribed to running magazines, read running books, visited running websites, and planned racing events to fuel my enthusiasm therefore my enthusiasm for the sport has endured.

My walk in faith with Jesus Christ has taken a similar route. Early in life, I was exposed to the Truth and for some time, was eager to learn more to fuel my enthusiasm for Christianity. My interest remained high as I attended parochial school and church on a regular basis and was surrounded by family and friends with similar interests.   During college, the flame of my enthusiasm remained lit but had dimmed significantly as lost much of my spiritual support system. The flame was reignited when I was exposed to followers who diligently studied the Word of God and applied their learning toward achieving contentment. The key to this renewed excitement in my faith as a Christian was fueling my interest through an environment that provided support. Joining and participating in a Bible-based church and small-group studies provided me with a deeper understanding of the message of the Good News of Jesus Christ. The things I learned and insights I gained further fueled my desire to learn more by studying the Bible on my own. Reading and contemplating the whole story of the Bible increased my understanding by filling in the gaps of messages that had previously been unclear.

As Jesus taught us in the Bible, faith without works can be empty promises. "What good is it, my brothers and sisters, if someone claims to have faith but does not have works? Can that faith save him? If a brother or sister is poorly clothed and lacking in daily food, and one of you says to them, *'Go in peace, be warmed and filled,'* without giving them the things they need for the body, what good is that?" *~James 2: 14-17*

The group of followers at our church continued to reinforce my faith by helping to spread the Word of God through mission trips, providing for the needy in our area, children's activities and prayer sessions. This increased focus on living my life to please the Lord barely repays His sacrifice of dying for all of the sins in the world, but has worked to bring me closer to Him.

To be the best that you can, fueling your soul with proper spiritual nutrition is equally important as physical nutrition. As in sport, providing fuel to strengthen and sustain your faith is nearly impossible to do without a credible support system. The best athletes seek out coaches, training partners, and published programs to educate, motivate, and support their goals.   The spiritual equivalent is to seek out mentors, peers, and the written Word to help us achieve a better understanding of the message of God.   After fasting for forty days, Jesus delivered the message of instructing us how to strengthen our faith. "Jesus answered," It is written: *'Man shall not live on bread alone, but on every word that comes from the mouth of God.'" ~Matthew 4:4.*

For man to excel in anything, whether athletic, academic, artistic or spiritual, you can only achieve your best if you fuel yourself properly.

Chapter Fourteen
Enjoying the Journey

"This is the day the LORD has made; let us rejoice and be glad in it." ~Psalm 118:24

The sunrise view was spectacular as we crested the top of the incline and began our descent down the bridge for the last 2 ½ miles of the five-mile run that spanned the Mackinaw Bridge. We glanced to the right and spotted Mackinaw Island amidst the crystal clear water. Since opening the bridge in 1957, the state of Michigan has hosted the annual Labor-Day Bridge Walk, a five mile trek that begins in the upper peninsula town of St. Ignace and ends on the shore of Mackinaw City. Prior to 1957, the State of Michigan was geographically divided into two distinct and separate worlds as the upper and lower- Peninsula were separated by the 5-mile long straights of Mackinaw that join the two great lakes, Huron, and Michigan. Prior to construction of the bridge, travelers regularly endured several hour delays to board the auto ferry that transported their vehicles and belongings to the wilderness of Michigan's Upper Peninsula. Even today, the construction of the Mackinaw Bridge is considered an incredible engineering feat as it took three years to complete at a cost of $100,000,000. Travelers are amazed at the sight of the main arch that rises two hundred feet and comes into view from several miles away. The bridge has no facilities for pedestrian traffic, so the Labor-Day walk has become the primary option for travelers who desire to experience the crossing on foot.

During the summer of 2008, I browsed the race flyers at the local running store and noticed an advertisement for a run across the bridge. According to the flyer, a lottery would be held to allow four hundred participants to run across the bridge prior to the 40,000 that would follow in the walk. Deb and I met the qualification of completing an approved event and decided to give it a shot. We were thrilled when the notice came that we had been accepted and we quickly made Northern Michigan camping plans for the holiday weekend. The experience included an early morning bus ride over the bridge to the start area, t-shirts, a welcome from the governor, and, of course, the run.

Despite the message that the run was non-competitive, Deb and I quickly made our way near the lead and as a result experience precious moments of solitude and quiet prior to the impending congestion that characterized later stages of the event. As I reflect back upon my years and adventures, this is one of many memorable moments that had become possible by my commitment to being a lifelong runner.

In the early spring of 2009, Deb and I embarked on another journey—a short trip to Utah, to run a half-marathon in the shadows of Arches National Park. As the crowd of runners stood on the scenic roadway, we knew there were just a few moments left before it was time to remove our sweatshirts and jackets and head to the starting line of the Canyonlands half marathon in Moab. I hesitated, waiting until the last minute as the thirty-seven degree temperature left me shivering. The sun rose and we knew that the air would quickly warm to an ideal temperature for our run. Deb and I drove with her sister Pat from Boulder, Colorado the night before and were now joined by several friends at the starting line.

The gun sounded and we headed out, running together at an honest but comfortable pace. The reddish cliffs that lined the roadway beamed with the reflection of the morning sun on our left. On the right, we could hear the rush of the rapids and see the glistening water of the Colorado River. The flat point-to-point course was closed to traffic for the duration of the race providing us with a feeling of peacefulness and solitude among a thousand other runners. When Deb and I approached the ten-mile mark, I realized my decision to wear a t-shirt was the right one as the temperature quickly rose to a comfortable sixty degrees. I quickly gulped water from the aid station and headed toward the finish line, determined to finish strong while remembering to enjoy the rest of the course. This was one of my favorite moments. The scenery of this run and many like it has become a wondrous memory, I recall numerous other moments where running made the experience even better. My running experiences include the grandeur of Yosemite Valley, the splendor of the Grand Canyon, the magnificence of Niagara Falls, and the peacefulness of the Great Smokey Mountains. While running, I have smelled the freshness of the ocean along Daytona Beach, Key West, San Francisco, and Malibu Beach. I intimately explored Main Street America by running through towns such as Akron, Ohio; Galena, Illinois; Elkhart, Indiana; McAlester, Oklahoma; Omaha, Nebraska; and Spokane, Washington. In Michigan, I have enjoyed sights such as the Sleeping Bear Sand Dunes in Traverse

City, Grand Island in Munising, Tahquamenon Falls, the Ludington lighthouse, and the Octagon Barn in Michigan's thumb. I have had the pleasure to support running events in both large and small towns across our state including the Peach Festival, Blueberry Festival, Sugar Beet Festival, and numerous other festival runs, each being characterized by their hospitality and uniqueness. My running adventures in Michigan have taken me to both Hell and Paradise.

Upon reflection about my running adventures, I quickly realized I didn't need to travel across the country to experience the wonders of nature but could cherish the environment right out my door. I could feel the same elation as I viewed Sunrise over Brendel Lake, a group of deer in the road, the scenery of deep woods, the landscape of country roads near my home. Like most runners, Deb and I have outlined and given names to the running routes that we frequent from our home. Each route offers the opportunity to gain new experiences as they are characterized by the differing terrain, distance, and scenery. The Hogback, City, Arboretum, and Huron Parkway loops all bring back memories of my favorite runs from my college days. Our current choices of home courses include the Porter Road, subdivision, high school, Pontiac Lake, Cooley Lake Road, Highland Rec, Indian Springs, and Whispering Meadows loops. Ask any runner and not only will they provide the course name, but the exact distance, terrain, best times, and other vital information about their routes. What this has taught me is that although I treasure the experiences of the great places I have been, I can find adventure and wonder right outside my door.

Late fall in 2009, I met Bob and Dave in the state park near my home and we were in the final stretches of a morning trail run. It was one of those days where we had to stop in our tracks and to admire the tunnel of golden trees that lined our route. The deep, blue, sky provided a perfect backdrop to the colorful foliage that encompassed the park. "It doesn't get any better than this," mentioned Bob as we resumed running up the next hill. The decades we all shared during our lifetime of running made us realize this is what running is all about.

****

Are you kidding me? "I'm a pretty good swimmer... and it doesn't look that far." My daughter Rose told the rest of us, hoping this day's journey would end sooner than later. After eight hours of hiking the rugged trails of Isle Royale in Lake Superior, we were tired and ready to call it a day. We reached the end of the trail that led to an inland bay of Lake Superior, separating us from our cabin on the other side. "This water isn't on the map." We concurred. We rested for a few minutes and weighed our options. On one hand, swimming looked attractive. However, the downsides were that few of us were good swimmers, the water was extremely cold, and we had plenty of gear we would have to leave. Our other option was to turn back on the path which meant an additional three hours to where we had turned onto the shortcut, and another two hours to our camp. It was already five o'clock and we would run the risk of being out in the wilderness after dark trying to traverse the hilly, rocky, and overgrown terrain. After deliberating, we decided if we jogged in stretches that were passable, we would get back to our cabin in three to four hours. Tired, hot, and thirsty we reluctantly began the trek home.

Our adventure to the island began early that morning in 2012 as Greg, Renee, Rachel, Rose, Deb, and I boarded the "Isle Royale Queen IV" for the three-hour boat ride from Michigan's northern most point in Copper Harbor. A morning storm made the ride a challenge and we were elated to see the clouds pass and feel the warmth of the sun as we landed at Rock Harbor, the island's only modern serviceable area. To call this area modern is a stretch as it consists of a small marina, gift shop, restaurant, six cabins, and the Rock Harbor Lodge. Other facilities on the island include shelters and tents for camping.

The 500,000 acre island was established as Isle Royale National Park by Franklin D. Roosevelt in 1940. The remoteness and wilderness adds to the intrigue and lure of the park but also contributes to it being the least visited park in the U.S. Its location, far from the shore of the mainland, limits the number of animal species that have made their way to it. The most common large mammals are moose and gray wolves. The island offers home to several smaller mammals including Isle Royale red squirrels, red foxes, river otters, mink, snowshoe hares, muskrats, beavers, and several bat species.

We neared our destination as dusk was settling in, tired, hungry, aching and thirsty and found the few places that served food were closed for the night. After a quick sigh, we went to plan B of raiding the pop machine and eating peanut butter and jelly sandwiches.   The next thing any of us recalled was awakening to the morning sun beaming through the cabin windows.

After a good night's sleep, we were re-energized and enjoyed stories and the details of our ordeal. Beyond the experience of our day-long hike, we recalled the beauty of the park, from the shores of Lake Superior, to the inland streams and lakes, to the fabulous view from the vista we had climbed to reach the highest point of the island. We boarded the ferry to Copper Harbor, and then we continued our adventures in Michigan's Upper Peninsula. We took in the beauty of the Porcupine Mountains, Pictured Rocks National Lakeshore, Presque Isle Park in Marquette, and numerous waterfalls. Our week-long trip provided us with several memorable views and moments as we stopped and took the time to marvel at the wonders of God's creations.

Whether we have been running, hiking, biking or traveling by vehicle, our family appreciated the magnificence of God's creations. From Acadia National Park in Maine to Key West, Florida, to the scenery along the Pacific Coast Highway, God gives us gifts that allow us to enjoy and appreciate His greatness. Standing next to the giant Redwoods in California, atop Mt. Evans in Colorado, or along the Atlantic Ocean in Savannah Georgia, I felt small yet in awe of the world in front of me.

As we enjoyed these journeys and marveled at the wonders of creation, our family has learned how God has empowered man as the most loved and cherished of His creations. *"Then God said, 'Let us make man in our image, after our likeness. And let them have dominion over the fish of the sea and over the birds of the heavens and over the livestock and over all the earth and over every creeping thing that creeps on the earth.' So God created man in His own image, in the image of God He created him; male and female He created them. And God blessed them. And God said to them, 'Be fruitful and multiply and fill the earth and subdue it, and have dominion over the fish of the sea and over the birds of the heavens and over every living thing that moves on the earth."* ~Genesis 1:26-28.

In our fallen world, man is destined to suffer and pay the price for sin. Despite the evil and suffering that are abundant in this life on earth we have hope for an eternal life through the sacrifice of Jesus Christ, our Savior. The Bible tells us in *Revelation 21:4* *"He will wipe away every tear from their eyes, and death shall be no more, neither shall there be mourning, nor crying, nor pain anymore, for the former things have passed away."*

For my entire life, I had searched for an answer to the question "What do I need to do to gain eternal life." I believed in God and in His Son Jesus Christ, who died to save us from sin, but still felt a need to understand more. When Jesus sacrificed himself, He provided us with the key to eternal life as taught to us in *John 3:16. "For God so loved the world that He gave His one and only Son, that whoever believes in Him shall not perish but have eternal life."*

"Can it be that simple?" I questioned. "All I have to do is believe?" We live in an imperfect world that is saddled with sin and suffering. It is impossible for any man to be sinless, but through further study I realized that good works are critical to please our Father.   He will forgive us if we confess our sins and are truly remorseful in our hearts, asking for His forgiveness and mercy. Obeying His great commandment as taught by Jesus in the Bible in a conversation with the Pharisees reveals what God requires from us. "Teacher, which is the great commandment in the Law?" And He said to him, *"You shall love the Lord your God with all your heart and with all your soul and with all your mind. This is the great and first commandment. And a second is like it: You shall love your neighbor as yourself.   On these two commandments depend all the Law and the Prophets." ~Matthew 22:36-40.*

I realized if I trusted in the Lord by putting my faith in the sacrifice of Jesus Christ as my Savior, my heart would be filled with the desire to please Him by obeying His command. My peace of mind came when I realized that good works alone will not gain my salvation but are the key to affirming our faith and trust in the Lord as these things go hand-in-hand

Jesus instructs us how to live our lives in the Sermon on the Mount: *"You are the light of the world. A city on a hill cannot be hidden. Nor do people light a lamp and put it under a basket, but on a stand, and it gives light to the whole house. In the same way, let your light shine before others so that they may see your good works and give glory to your Father who is in heaven." Matthew 5:14-16.*

Through my understanding of God's message, I have gained the strength of knowing I can overcome all trials and tribulation. I put my faith in God's provision for my salvation, and even though there is nothing I can do on my own, I will do my best to please Him by fulfilling His command and spreading the Good News to my brothers. As I continue my worldly journey, I no longer count on myself to gain God's approval. Instead, I continually seek ways to reaffirm my faith and heed His command. In my quest to gain eternal happiness with my savior, I understand that through faith in Jesus I'm already there.

Connecting with Others

Thinking back to my early days as a runner, I recalled the inspiration I felt from watching my senior teammates, high school champions, and nationally-ranked distance runners compete in track and field and road racing. They motivated me to run and compete throughout my life. Little did I dream that my decision to run would similarly affect so many others to do the same. Those inspired are not only those who I know but are expanded to friends of friends and more. I would like to believe that my decision to become a runner has led others to a more fulfilling life. Much like the inspiration I drew upon from the elite runners of my youth, I sense that I have either directly or indirectly inspired hundreds to give it a try. From the high-schoolers I coached to my family, friends, co-workers, and teammates, my life has been enhanced by sharing the gift of running with them.

My decision to run has introduced me to new friends, taken me many places, and allowed me to share more of my life with my family and friends. It has strengthened my character by teaching me the need for patience, perseverance, dedication, and commitment. Running has given me confidence by allowing me to achieve much more in life than I thought was possible. Most importantly I have learned that attaining my goals, although satisfying is not as important or rewarding as the journey I have taken.

I am similarly appreciative of the people who have inspired me to pursue my spiritual faith. The examples, instruction, and motivation provided by fellow Christians have deeply impacted me to actively pursue Jesus Christ as my Savior. As the Christian faith has taken hold of my life, I aim to strengthen and support others as I humbly spread the Good News of Jesus Christ. As others grow in faith, Gods' desire to share eternal happiness with all of creation will be realized.

Conclusion

What's Next

"But seek first his kingdom and his righteousness, and all these things will be given to you as well." ~Matthew 6:33

It's Not About The Race, But About The Journey. This phrase sums up what I have found to be the key to contentment and happiness. Through the process of writing this book, I discovered my life's purpose by understanding where I came from, where I am at, and where I want to be.

Whether sharing thoughts with others, reflecting on your own, praying to the Lord, or writing your own story, I urge you to step back and answer these three critical questions to find your purpose and contentment.

1. Where did I come from?

2. Where am I at?

3. Where do I want to be?

     Writing this book provided me with valuable memories of my life and helped me reflect upon the lessons I learned. I learned to become the person I want to be by working through pain, uncertainty, heartache, barriers, and difficulties. I learned to rejoice in the memories of joyful times, relationships, successes, and good times. Most importantly, I gained a new perspective that what is truly important is living my life to seek to understand Gods' message and continue to work to establish a meaningful relationship with our Father. Whether you are confused, lost and seeking contentment or confident in your direction in life, knowing what is important and embracing a lifestyle to support it is the essential first step.

     Although this book focuses on the parallels to achieving contentment with our running and spiritual life, it is essential for you to recognize the highest priority must be living your life for Christ, accepting His sacrifice of dying on the cross will provide you with eternal salvation, and contentment in worldly things such as running are merely gifts from God. Therefore in any achievements you attain, you must give thanks and glory to Him rather than pride and honor to yourself.

     I have personally found that the following principles have guided me to the state of contentment and peace. I urge you to reflect upon these principles as you begin your evaluation.

1.   You are one of a kind. You are a unique individual unlike anyone else who has ever walked on the earth. Your likes, dislike, talents, and personality are unlike anyone else's.   As you reflect upon your goals and experiences, remember that motivation needs to come from within rather than from the expectations of others.

2.   Remember your purpose. As believers in Jesus Christ, the guiding principle of your faith and purpose is to live your life to glorify God who created all things and through the sacrifice of His Son wants you to share eternal happiness with Him.

3.   Put others first.   Next to putting God first, Jesus instructs us to love and support one another by putting the needs of others before our own. As you live your life to support those in need, you will learn that the focus of your personal troubles is lessened and replaced with the satisfaction of helping one another.

4.   Attitude is everything. Jesus taught us that praying without action is meaningless. If you truly embrace the core of our faith... that Jesus Christ paid the ultimate price by suffering and dying for the sins of the world, you will live your life with an attitude and actions that are pleasing to Him.

5.   Seek to understand. To get the most out of your daily activities it is critical you understand and embrace what you are doing rather than going through the motions. Understanding fulfills one of the major needs of humankind- purpose.

6.   Listen to your body and heart. Let your heart and spirit guide you through life's challenges as you enhance your relationship with Jesus. Do not let outsiders influence your decisions. Your mind and body will let you know when to relax and refresh your physical and inner self.

7.   Embrace the Ultimate Sacrifice. Christianity teaches us the only way to eternal happiness with the Father is through faith that Jesus Christ died to avenge the sins of mankind. Being a good person and obeying the teachings of Jesus alone will not suffice to pay for the sinful nature of mankind. However; living a life that is pleasing to God and seeking God's forgiveness when you stumble will draw you closer to Him and reward you with joy and contentment.

8.   Do the Work. Achieving your athletic and spiritual goals requires strengthening your mind and body for ultimate performance. The benefits of strong faith, the proper attitude, motivation, and recovery can only be maximized if you work diligently to understand, plan, and then do the work needed to strengthen yourself.

9.   Embrace the Journey. You cannot reach a goal unless you set it. However, every minute of our lives will be enhanced if you take the time to slow down, reflect, and enjoy where you are at any given time. Your mortal existence should drive you to appreciate each moment and breath that has been provided by our Creator.

James Deren

This is the story of a runner and athlete related to his Christian growth. It is a narrative recounting 115,000 running miles, enough to circle the earth five times, and the correlation of finding faith in everyday life.

The author's journey took him from life as an average athlete and casual Christian, to many experiences and accomplishments- both spiritually and physically.   The message is to treasure the experiences along the way to goals.

The author is part of the baby-boomer generation, born in the 1950's and growing up in a simple, middle-class environment. He progressed from an average high-school runner to a two-time All-American in the mile run and captain of nationally ranked, college track and cross-country teams, with a personal best of 4:01 in the mile. He has raced against, beaten, and become friends with, Olympians and World-Record holders such as Marty Liquori, Rod Dixon, Dick Quax, Steve Scott, Greg Meyer, Herb Lindsay, Eamonn Coghlin, Paul Cummings, Wilson Waigwa and Steve Placencia. He's had both national and local sponsorships and attracted media attention including being featured on Wide World of Sports, ESPN, WJR Radio and CBS.

Later in life, the transition to road racing resulted in a sub-thirty-minute 10K, sub-fourteen-minute 5K and 2:29 marathon. He continues to be an active member of the running community through memberships on running teams, trail relay and events, and family running events. Through running experiences, he established relationships with thousands of friends and dozens of close companions. He seeks out new adventures such as triathlons. His journey includes growth as a Christian from a traditional parochial school upbringing in the 1960's to a life that revolves around our Savior Jesus Christ. After more than forty years of attending Sunday Service, he pursues being an everyday Christian through small groups, volunteer work, daily prayer, and studying the Bible.

Follow James Deren at www.run2faith.com.

42183091R00104

Made in the USA
Lexington, KY
11 June 2015